HIGH SCHOOL
TALKSHEETS

50 READY-TO-USE DISCUSSIONS
ON THE LIFE OF CHRIST

TERRY LINHART

ZONDERVAN®

ZONDERVAN.com/
AUTHORTRACKER
follow your favorite authors

youth
specialties

**youth
specialties**

High School Talksheets: 50 Ready-to-Use Discussions on the Life of Christ
Copyright 2009 by Terry Linhart

Youth Specialties resources, 300 S. Pierce St., El Cajon, CA 92020 are published by Zondervan, 5300 Patterson Ave. SE, Grand Rapids, MI 49530.

ISBN 978-0-310-28552-6

Cover design by David Conn
Interior design by Brandi Etheredge Design

Printed in the United States of America

09 10 11 12 13 14 15 16 • 20 19 18 17 16 15 14 13 12 11 10 9 8 7 6 5 4 3 2 1

No book project is produced alone, and I need to acknowledge those at YS who made this piece better than I could have imagined. I am grateful to Dave Urbanski for his gracious editing and wonderful humor. To Jay, Roni, and Mindi—thanks for keeping me focused and productive. To Jen, Lorna, Dan, Welch, Mindi, Dave, David, Amy, Andy, Janie, and Brandi—thank you for your gifts and diligence. Thanks also to Bethel College students Holly Birkey, Tom Carpenter, and Danno Lambert for their contributions, and to Jenna Yabsley for her early feedback. Special thanks to Kelly, my best friend and partner in life, for her editorial reviews and encouragement along the way.

CONTENTS

THE HOWS AND WHATS OF TALKSHEETS

High School TalkSheets—The Life of Christ contains 50 discussions that focus on the major events and teachings in Jesus' life…and some that your students may have never encountered before. Each of the 50 discussions includes a reproducible TalkSheet for your students to work on, as well as simple, step-by-step instructions on how to use it. All you need is this book, some Bibles, a few copies of the handouts, and some kids (some food won't hurt, either). Then you're on your way to helping your students discover more about the life of Christ.

These TalkSheets are user-friendly and very flexible. They can be used in youth group meetings, Sunday school classes, or in Bible study groups. You can adapt them for either large or small groups. And they can be covered in only 20 minutes or explored more intensively. You can build an entire youth group meeting around a single TalkSheet, or you can use TalkSheets to supplement other materials and resources you might be covering. This will be a book you'll keep using for many years as you help kids learn more about Christ.

LEADING A TALKSHEET DISCUSSION

TalkSheets can be used as a curriculum for your youth group, but they're designed as springboards for discussion. They encourage your kids to take part and interact with each other while talking about key stories from the life of Christ. And hopefully they'll do some serious thinking, discover new ideas, defend their points of view, and make decisions.

Youth today live in an active world that bombards them with the voices of society and the media—most of which drown out what they hear from the church. Youth leaders must teach the church's beliefs and values—and help young people make the right choices in a world full of options. The stories and themes from the life of Christ are central to helping your high school students understand their faith.

A TalkSheet discussion works for this very reason. While dealing with the questions and activities on the TalkSheet, your kids will think carefully about issues, compare their beliefs and values with others and with Scripture, and make their own choices. TalkSheets will challenge your group to explain and rework their ideas in a Christian atmosphere of acceptance, support, and growth.

Maybe you're asking yourself, *What will I do if the kids in my group just sit there and don't say anything?* Well, when kids don't have anything to say, a lot of times it's because they haven't had a chance or time to get their thoughts organized. Most young people haven't developed the ability to think on their feet. Since many are afraid they might sound stupid, they often avoid voicing their ideas and opinions.

The solution? TalkSheets let your kids deal with the issues in a challenging but nonthreatening way before the actual discussion begins. They'll have time to organize their thoughts, write them down, and ease their fears about participating. They may even look forward to sharing their answers. Most importantly, they'll want to find out what others said and open up to talk through the topics from the life of Christ.

If you're still a little leery about leading a discussion with your kids, that's okay—the only way to get them rolling is to get them started.

YOUR ROLE AS THE LEADER

The best discussions don't happen by accident. They require careful preparation and a sensitive, enthusiastic, and caring leader. Don't worry if you aren't experienced or don't have hours to prepare. TalkSheets are designed to help even the novice leader. The more TalkSheet discussions you lead, the easier it becomes. So keep the following tips in mind when using the TalkSheets as you get your kids talking:

BE CHOOSY

Each TalkSheet deals with a different story from the life of Christ. Choose a TalkSheet based on the needs and the maturity level of your group. Don't feel obligated to use the TalkSheets in the order they appear in this book. Use your best judgment and mix them up any way you want. However, they are roughly arranged in a chronological timeline, so you can focus on a period in Jesus' life, or you can get four or five together for a month's series on a theme or time period.

TRY IT YOURSELF

Once you've chosen a TalkSheet for your group, answer the questions and do the activities yourself. Though each TalkSheet session has a similar structure, they each contain different activities. Imagine your kids' reactions to the TalkSheet. This will help you prepare for the discussion and understand what you're asking them to do. Plus, you'll have some time to think of other appropriate questions, activities, and Bible verses that help tailor it to your kids.

GET SOME INSIGHT

On each leader's guide page, you'll find numerous tips and ideas for getting the most out of your dis-

cussion. You may want to add some of your own thoughts or ideas in the margins. And there's room to keep track of the date and the name of your group at the top of the leader's page. You'll also find suggestions for additional activities and discussion questions.

There are some references to Internet links throughout the TalkSheets. These are guides for you to find the resources and information you need. For additional help, be sure to visit the Youth Specialties Web site at www.YouthSpecialties.com for information on materials and other links for finding what you need. Be careful as you use the Internet and videos—you'll need to (carefully!) preview them first (if applicable, you might need to check with your supervisor if you aren't sure if they're appropriate) and try to avoid any surprises.

MAKE COPIES

Your students will need their own copies of the TalkSheet—but make sure you only make copies of the student's side of the TalkSheet. The material on the reverse side (the leader's guide) is just for you. Remember: You're permitted to make copies for your group because we've said you can—but just for your youth group…not for every youth group in your state! U.S. copyright laws haven't changed, and it's still mandatory to request permission before making copies of published material. Thank you for cooperating.

INTRODUCE THE TOPIC

It's important to have a definite starting point to your session and introduce the topic before you pass out your TalkSheets to your group. Depending on your group, keep it short and to the point. Be careful to avoid over-introducing the topic, sounding preachy, or resolving the issue before you've started. Your goal is to spark your students' interest and leave plenty of room for discussion. You may also want to tell a story, share an experience, or describe a situation or problem having to do with the topic. You might want to jump-start your group by asking something like, "What's the first thing you think of when you hear the word _____ [insert the word here]?" After a few answers, you can add something like, "Well, it seems we all have different ideas about this subject. Tonight we're going to investigate it a bit further…"

The following are excellent methods you can use to introduce any lesson in this book—

• Show a related short film or video.
• Read a passage from a book or magazine that relates to the subject.
• Play a popular song that deals with the topic.
• Perform a short skit or dramatic presentation.
• Play a simulation game or role-play, setting up the topic.
• Present current statistics, survey results, or read a newspaper article that provides recent information about the topic.
• Use posters, videos, or other visuals to help focus attention on the topic.

THE OPENER

We've designed the OPENER to be a great kick-off to the discussion. Some may work better to use **before** you pass out the TalkSheets. Others may work better as discussion starters **after** the students have completed their TalkSheets. You decide! Check out the MORE section, too—it often contains an alternate opening idea or activity that'll help get students upbeat and talking, which is perfect for leading an effective TalkSheet discussion. TIP: When you're leading a game or OPENER, consider leading it like a game-show host would. Now that may not sound very spiritual, but if you think about what a host does (builds goodwill,

creates excitement, facilitates community, listens to others) that sounds pretty pastoral, doesn't it? Plus, it makes it more fun!

ALLOW ENOUGH TIME

Pass out copies of the TalkSheet to your kids after the OPENER and make sure each person has a pen or pencil and a Bible. There are usually four to six discussion activities on each TalkSheet. If your time is limited, or if you're using only a part of the TalkSheet, tell the group to complete only the activities you'd like them to complete.

Decide ahead of time if you'd like your students to work on the TalkSheets individually or in groups. Sometimes the TalkSheet will already have students working in small groups. Let them know how much time they have for completing the TalkSheet, then again when there's a minute (or so) left. Go ahead and give them some extra time and then start the discussion when everyone seems ready to go.

SET UP FOR THE DISCUSSION

Make sure the seating arrangement is inclusive and encourages a comfortable, safe atmosphere for discussion. Theater-style seating (in rows) isn't discussion-friendly. Instead, arrange the chairs in a circle or semicircle (or sit on the floor with pillows!).

SET BOUNDARIES

It'll be helpful to set a few ground rules before the discussion. Keep the rules to a minimum, of course, but let the kids know what's expected of them. Here are suggestions for some basic ground rules—

• **What's said in this room stays in this room.** Emphasize the importance of confidentiality. Confidentiality is vital for a good discussion. If your kids can't keep the discussion in the room, then they won't open up.

- **No put-downs.** Mutual respect is important. If your kids disagree with some opinions, ask them to comment on the subject (but not on the other person). It's okay to have healthy debate about different ideas, but personal attacks aren't kosher—and they detract from discussion. Communicate that your students can share their thoughts and ideas—even if they may be different or unpopular.
- **There's no such thing as a dumb question.** Your group members must feel free to ask questions at any time. In fact, since *High School TalkSheets—The Life of Christ* digs into a lot of Scripture, you may get hard questions from students that you cannot immediately answer. DON'T PANIC! Affirm that it's a great question, and you aren't sure of the answer—but you'll do some study over the next week and unpack it next time (and be sure to do this).
- **No one is forced to talk.** Some kids will open up, some won't. Let everyone know they each have the right to pass or not answer any question.
- **Only one person speaks at a time.** This is a mutual respect issue. Everyone's opinion is worthwhile and deserves to be heard.

Communicate with your group that everyone needs to respect these boundaries. If you sense your group members are attacking each other or adopting a negative attitude during the discussion, stop and deal with the problem before going on. Every youth ministry needs to be a safe place where students can freely be who God created them to be without fear.

SET THE STAGE

Always phrase your questions so that you're asking for an opinion, not a be-all, end-all answer. The simple addition of the less-threatening "What do you think…" at the beginning of a question makes it a request for an opinion rather than a demand for the right answer. Your kids will relax when they feel more comfortable and confident. Plus, they'll know you actually care about their opinions, and they'll feel appreciated.

LEAD THE DISCUSSION

Discuss the TalkSheet with the group and encourage all your kids to participate. The more they contribute, the better the discussion will be.

If your youth group is big, you may divide it into smaller groups. Some of the TalkSheets request that your students work in smaller groups. Once the smaller groups have completed their discussions, combine them into one large group and ask the different groups to share their ideas.

You don't have to divide the group with every TalkSheet. For some discussions you may want to vary the group size or divide the meeting into groups of the same sex. The discussion should target the questions and answers on the TalkSheet. Go through them and ask the students to share their responses. Have them compare their answers and brainstorm new ones in addition to the ones they've written down.

AFFIRM ALL RESPONSES— RIGHT OR WRONG

Let your kids know that their comments and contributions are appreciated and important. This is especially true for those who rarely speak during group activities. Make a point of thanking them for joining in. This will be an incentive for them to participate further.

Remember that affirmation doesn't mean approval. Affirm even those comments that seem wrong to you. You'll show that everyone has a right to express ideas—no matter how controversial those ideas may be. If someone states an off-base opinion, make a mental note of the comment. Then in your wrap-up, come back to the comment or present a different point of view in a positive way. But don't reprimand the student who voiced the comment.

AVOID GIVING THE AUTHORITATIVE ANSWER

Some kids believe you have the correct answer to every question. They'll look to you for approval, even when they're answering another group member's question. If they start to focus on you for answers, redirect them toward the group by making a comment like, "Remember that you're talking to everyone, not just me."

LISTEN TO EACH PERSON

Good discussion leaders know how to listen. Although it's tempting at times, don't monopolize the discussion. Encourage others to talk first—then express your opinions during your wrap-up.

DON'T FORCE IT

Encourage all your kids to talk, but don't make them comment. Each member has the right to pass. If you feel that the discussion isn't going well, go to the next question or restate the present question to keep things moving.

DON'T TAKE SIDES

Encourage everybody to think through their positions and opinions—ask questions to get them going deeper. If everyone agrees on an issue, you can play devil's advocate with tough questions and stretch their thinking. Remain neutral—your point of view is your own, not that of the group.

DON'T LET ANYONE (INCLUDING YOU) TAKE OVER

Nearly every youth group has one person who likes to talk and is perfectly willing to express an opinion on any subject—*all the time.* Encourage equal participation from all members.

LET THEM LAUGH!

Discussions can be fun! Most of the TalkSheets include questions that'll make students laugh and get them thinking, too. Some of your students' answers will be hilarious—feel free to stop and laugh as a group.

LET THEM BE SILENT

Silence can be scary for discussion leaders! Some react by trying to fill the silence with a question or a comment. The following suggestions may help you to handle silence more effectively—

- **Be comfortable with silence.** Wait it out for 30 seconds or so to respond, which can feel like forever in a group. You may want to restate the question to give your kids a gentle nudge.
- **Talk about the silence with the group.** What does the silence mean? Do they really not have any comments? Maybe they're confused, embarrassed, or don't want to share.
- **Answer the silence with questions or comments like, "I know this is challenging to think about..." or "It's scary to be the first to talk."** If you acknowledge the silence, it may break the ice.
- **Ask a different question that may be easier to handle or that'll clarify the one already posed.** But don't do this too quickly without giving them time to think the first one through.
- **The "two more answers" key.** When you feel like moving on from a question, you may want to ask for two more answers to make sure you've heard all of the great ideas. Many students have good

stuff to say, but for one reason or another choose not to share. This key skill may help you draw out some of the best answers before moving on.

KEEP IT UNDER CONTROL

Monitor the discussion. Be aware if the discussion is going in a certain direction or off track. This can happen fast, especially if your students disagree or things get heated. Mediate wisely and set the tone that you want. If your group gets bored with an issue, get them back on track. Let the discussion unfold but be sensitive to your group and who is or isn't getting involved.

If a student brings up a side issue that's interesting, decide whether or not to pursue it. If the discussion is going well and the issue is worth discussing, let them talk it through. But if things get off track, say something like, "Let's come back to that subject later if we have time. Right now, let's finish our discussion on..."

BE CREATIVE AND FLEXIBLE

If you find other ways to use the TalkSheets, use them! Go ahead and add other questions or Bible references. Don't feel pressured to spend time on every single activity. If you're short on time, you can skip some items. Stick with the questions that are the most interesting to the group.

SET YOUR GOALS

TalkSheets are designed to move along toward a goal, but you need to identify *your* goal in advance. What would you like your youth to learn? What truth should they discover? What's the goal of the session? If you don't know where you're going, it's doubtful you'll get there.

BE THERE FOR YOUR KIDS

Some kids may actually want to talk more with you about a certain topic. (Hey! You got 'em thinking!) Let them know you can talk one-on-one with them afterward.

CLOSE THE DISCUSSION

Present a challenge to the group by asking yourself, "What do I want my students to remember most from this discussion?" There's your wrap-up! It's important to conclude by affirming the group and offering a summary that ties the discussion together.

Sometimes you won't need a wrap-up. You may want to leave the issue hanging and discuss it in another meeting. That way, your group can think about it more and you can nail down the final ideas later.

TAKE IT FURTHER

On the leader's guide page, you'll find additional materials—labeled MORE—that provide extra assistance to you. Some sessions contain an additional activity—i.e., an opener, expanded discussion, or fun idea. Some have support material that can help you handle some potential confusion related to the topic. These aren't a must, but highly recommended. They let the kids reflect upon, evaluate, dig in a bit more, review, and assimilate what they've learned. These activities may lead to even more discussion and better learning.

A FINAL WORD

My goal in writing this TalkSheet book was to help your students grow in their understanding of the Bible, the richness of the stories from the life of Christ—and to learn more about who Jesus is and his invitation to follow him. The bottom line is to have fun teaching your students from the life of Christ.

1. Imagine what it will be like to live in your neighborhood or city 100 years from now. Write down three predictions you have about what your neighborhood will be like.

2. Team up with three other people and have each person pick one Bible passage. Read them out loud and discuss the difference between a prediction and a prophecy. As a group, write a sentence that summarizes your answer to what makes them different.

a. Deuteronomy 18:22

b. 2 Chronicles 36:15

c. Isaiah 45:21

d. 2 Peter 1:20, 21

3. People expected the Messiah (John 1:41) because they knew about the prophecies in the Old Testament. As a group, discuss these prophecies and draw a line from each prophecy to its completion in the life of Jesus.

Isaiah 7:14   The Messiah would be born in Bethlehem. (Matthew 2:6)
Isaiah 9:7   The Messiah would enter Jerusalem on a donkey. (Matthew 21:1-11)
Zechariah 9:9   His name was Immanuel, which means "God with us." (Matthew 1:23)
Micah 5:2   He would be a descendant of King David. (Matthew 1:1-6)

4. Both Jesus and Peter draw attention to Old Testament prophecies. Each group member should pick one of the following verses and rewrite it in his or her own words.

Luke 24:44

Acts 10:43

5. After reading some of the prophecies predicting the Messiah, check the statement that best expresses your response.

___ I have new confidence in the Bible.
___ How could people not know who Jesus was?
___ I need to check this out some more.
___ I can see how people gave up hope for a Messiah after waiting so long.
___ I wish someone could tell me what my future holds.

THIS WEEK

When studying the life of Christ, it's important to consider the perspectives of those in the stories. It's important to know the context of whatever passage or theme you're studying in the Bible. This lesson helps set the context for the life of Christ, focusing on the prophecies in the Old Testament that point to the coming Messiah. This TalkSheet exposes students to these key passages of Scripture, shows how the prophecies were fulfilled in the life of Christ, and prompts students to think about the authority of Scripture for their lives.

OPENER

To get students oriented toward the topic, ask, "What are the *kinds* of predictions you've heard people make? You may have heard people give them, read them somewhere, or watched someone give them on TV." After a minute of this discussion, ask quick responses on whether these predictions came true or not (don't write these down—just get the students sharing rapid answers). Without letting that drag on too long, use a whiteboard or newsprint to write answers to this question: "What are some *specific* predictions you've recently heard about the future?" If students struggle, you can suggest categories—relationships at school, environmental issues, politics, future jobs, sports, and the end times. After you've written these (and make sure you ask for two more answers when you want to end this opening discussion—these last couple of answers are often some of the better answers in discussions), you can have students rate the likelihood of each of these happening on a scale of 1 to 5 with 5 being most likely. Don't let this drag—keep it moving!

Ask students what factors influenced their ratings and write their answers to this question in another column or on more newsprint. Transition into the TalkSheet portion by telling students there were numerous predictions, some very detailed, about Jesus' birth, life, death, and resurrection. This TalkSheet will discuss some of those and help us consider the role Scripture plays in our life.

DISCUSSION

1. Most people think about the future and make plans as if it's going to go the way they imagine. But life isn't predictable. Have students share the best of their predictions with someone near them. Did some predictions seem more likely than others?

2. True prophecy in the Bible came from God through true prophets. With so many false prophets and false messiahs during the days of Scripture, how could people tell the true ones from the false ones?

3. Ask the students: "If you were living in the time of Christ, which of these four would you have found the most amazing to see fulfilled?" Why? If there's time, explore reasons why people didn't recognize Jesus as Messiah.

4. Have a few students share what they wrote. Make sure to get several responses for each verse, and give students who normally don't get to respond a chance to do so here.

5. It may be important to tell students that *no* prophecy about who the Messiah would be and what he'd do *wasn't* fulfilled in the life of Jesus Christ.

CLOSE

Summarize how prophecy written hundreds of years before Christ was fulfilled. Build on the discussion from question #3 and remind students that some Old Testament prophecy about the second coming of Jesus is still to happen. Have students briefly share whether or not these prophecies make any difference in the lives of people today. Fulfilled prophecy in the Bible reminds us of its authority in our lives, even when people may choose to ignore it. Following Jesus means we should seek to understand his life and teachings in the Bible. What commitments can we make to learn more about Jesus and allow him to lead our lives?

MORE

• **It may be worth it to provide a handout for students detailing Old Testament prophecies and their relationship to the life of Christ. Make sure this is formatted well and looks sharp, and consider limiting it to the 10 you believe are most significant.**

• **The Bible can be intimidating to read. Discuss this with your students: How are they doing with reading and understanding God's Word? You may want to develop a reading schedule for them, one that parallels this TalkSheet book or one that helps them read through particular books of the Bible. Or consider forming a Bible-reading club so students can encourage each other and discuss their readings online or in person.**

THE PRAYER OF A TEENAGER

Mary's prayer

(Luke 1:26-38; 46-55)

1. When do you pray the "best"? You know, those times God seems close when you pray, and you pray as if you're sure God is listening. Put a "B" beside all that apply below. Now go back through the list below and put an X beside those times when you probably don't pray very much at all.

____ When I'm hurting	____ At church
____ When things are going well	____ Before big events
____ With friends	____ When I need help
____ In the summer	____ When I'm joyful
____ During school	____ For schoolwork
____ With my family	____ When I'm confident
____ On vacation	____ When I'm fearful
	____ Some other time

2. Do you—or does someone in your family—have a set prayer at meals or at night? If so, write down a few of the phrases you remember from that prayer:

3. Have students get in a group with two or three others and have one person in each group read Hannah's prayer in 1 Samuel 2:1-10 out loud. Have another person follow that by reading Mary's prayer in Luke 1:46-55. Write down any phrases or ideas that appear in both prayers.

4. In the face of such a life-changing event, Mary's response to the angel's declaration (verse 38) was simply, "I am the Lord's servant. May it be to me according to your word." (NIV) List two or three areas of your life where it is difficult to trust God and simply obey.

Would it be easier to obey if an angel showed up in your bedroom and told you that God really wanted you to just trust him in these areas?

Why?

5. Look over your answers to the previous question and consider the ways in which you've prayed about them. If someone saw your answers, how would they describe them?

THIS WEEK

Some teenagers have mature prayer lives that most adults know nothing about. They're meaningful times that can have profound effects in high schoolers' lives. One of the most beautiful prayers in all of Scripture is the prayer of a teenager—Mary. Her response to the angel when she was told she'd give birth to the Messiah is a rich section of Scripture for students to encounter. This TalkSheet exposes students to Mary's prayer and to Mary the teenager—and it offers students an opportunity to reflect on and share about their own prayer practices.

OPENER

Before your meeting, enlarge and copy Luke 1:26-38—one for every five students. Write out the verse numbers and cut the verses into strips and put each set into a separate envelope. Keep a bag of candy on hand as a small prize.

Tell students to get in groups of five to six and then hand an envelope to each group. Each group has the story of the angel visiting Mary, but they have to put the verses in order. The first group to do so will win a fabulous prize (that they will then share with everyone else). You'll need multiple adult judges available to review the groups' efforts and award a winner. Give the bag of candy to the winning group—and encourage them to share!

Tell students you're going to read through Mary's prayer in Luke 1:46-55 and that you want them to change their posture (stand or sit down) whenever you read something Mary says about what God has done. If they're sitting, they'll stand. If standing, they'll sit. After you're done, ask students if anyone kept track of how many times they changed position during Mary's prayer. *(The answer should be eight.)*

DISCUSSION

1. After students have worked through these, read through them one by one and ask students to report by raising their hands when their answer is read. They're not to comment, just to raise their hands so everyone can visually contribute to the discussion. Afterward ask, "Which of the options marked were you most sure about?"

2. Is it okay to say the same prayer before each meal, or should people make up a new one each time? Do your students notice a connection between the times when they don't pray much and when they pray best?

3. Note to the students that Mary was strong in her faith in God. Her prayer shows her knowledge of the Old Testament and how the Messiah would establish his earthly kingdom. Ask students how they've grown in their knowledge of the Bible and who Jesus is. You can list these on the board or newsprint. Ask, "How did you learn to pray?" This question gets more specific and helps show

the ways significant role models can help us grow in our spiritual lives.

4. Sometimes it's hard to trust that God is capable of doing big things. Mary evidently understood what God was capable of doing—challenging the rulers of the world and lifting up those who were poor but who trusted in him. Why is it sometimes difficult to pray as if we really know God is capable of answering our prayers? What qualities does Mary the teenager model?

5. Mary was overcome when she realized the God of Scripture had taken notice of her, and she understood the important role she was about to play. Remind students that God continually notices us (Matthew 10:29, 30), but we can often feel very distant from him. Have a few students share the descriptive words they wrote. Ask students with positive descriptions to give an example of how they came up with it. Do this with two or three students.

CLOSE

Mary's prayer reveals much about her knowledge of Scripture, her awareness of who God is, and her willingness to obey God. Our prayer practices often reveal the nature of our relationship with God—and our level of trust in him. How do our prayer lives connect with how we live for God? Is there a connection? What if someone read our prayers as we can do with Mary's—what would they observe? Have your students write down two things they can do this week to strengthen their prayer lives.

MORE

• **You may want to consider organizing a prayer emphasis for your youth group. Will your students pray for 24 hours straight? Divide the 24 hours into equal time slots and have them sign up for those times. Students can come pray at the church or another building, or pray at home. Whenever possible, it's best to hold your prayer vigil at a single location.**
• **Some youth groups have held a prayer chain for one week—and numerous churches have done it for a whole year. You may want to consider creating a prayer room where students can write prayers and post them on the wall or read the Bible and prayerful devotional readings. Decorate the room, add some candles, be creative, and put a vibrant visual emphasis on prayer. (*Sacred Space* by Dan Kimball and Lilly Lewin is all about creating such prayer environments.)**
• **Have students spend time in silence and reflection to create some quiet space. You could play some soft, reflective instrumental worship music. As students listen in the quiet, have a female student with a good voice read Mary's prayer. Give students a minute or two of silence to absorb the prayer, then have the student read it once more. Close with a short prayer that your students will reflect the goodness of God and the hope of Jesus Christ in their lives this week.**

1. Were there moments when you realized you were no longer a little kid anymore? Write down as many as you can think of.

2. Leviticus 12:1-8 describes what Mary and Joseph were doing in this story. Read it, and then compare verse 8 with Luke 2:24. What do you learn about Mary and Joseph's social status from these verses?

The sacrifice is for purification. This isn't a word we hear very often. Imagine you're explaining what it means to be made pure to a fourth-grader. What three words or phrases would you use?

3. When you're old and look back on your life, what values will you believe are most important? Check the three most important observations you'd wish for when looking back:

_____ I had a happy life.   _____ I had a successful career.

_____ My family was happy.   _____ I had a healthy life.

_____ I got to take cool vacations.   _____ I had some nice cars.

_____ I followed Jesus faithfully.   _____ I made a lot of money.

_____ I had a deep relationship with God.   _____ I made a difference in the world.

_____ I got to do what I wanted to do.   _____ Other _____

4. Simeon was described as "righteous" and "devout." Describe someone you know who has godly character:

How would others describe your character?

____ It's difficult for them to see the real me.   _____ My character doesn't match who I am.

____ They can easily see my commitment.   _____ I'm an average person.

____ I really need to work on this area.

5. **God showed his faithfulness to Simeon and Anna as they showed their faithfulness to God. List two areas where you can be faithful to and show trust in God.**

THIS WEEK

In the early days of Jesus' life, we read short stories that show us a glimpse of the significance that Jesus as Messiah held for God's faithful. Though Jesus was fully God, it's equally important to note that Jesus was fully human. This TalkSheet allows students to see the faithfulness of God through the eyes of Simeon and Anna and exposes students to the religious background in which Jesus was raised.

OPENER

Ask students to define *rite of passage*. What major moments do we encounter on the way to being an adult woman or man? On a whiteboard or newsprint easel up front, write students' answers bottom to top, with the earliest "major moments" at the bottom. (Some might mention potty training or tying a shoe while others might mention events connected to church.) The goal is to get your students talking about growing up. Some may notice that their upbringing didn't have many rites of passage. Tell students you're now going to look at a story from early in Jesus' life.

Preselect two students and ask them ahead of time to read. You read Luke 1:22-24. Then have the male student read Luke 1:25-32 and the female student read Luke 1:33-39.

DISCUSSION

1. Have them turn to someone nearby and share what they wrote. After three minutes, ask for volunteers to share examples with the larger group. Did some students have similar answers?
2. Mary and Joseph were probably quite poor (Leviticus 12:8). Jesus and his parents followed the requirements of the Law so he could fulfill the law—could offer grace and forgiveness to us as well as adoption (Galatians 4:4) into his family as God's children (John 1:12-13). Ask your students if they think of themselves as being "God's kid." Should they? Would it have an effect on what they do?
3. Discuss these answers with your students. How do these values mirror their current values? Have them think of older people they know and share what seem to be important values to those people. Are they similar to or different from their own answers? Simeon and Anna were devout Israelite believers—examples of the best of those faithful to God throughout the Old Testament time.
4. The words *righteous* and *devout* could be given to any of them. After hundreds of years of waiting, people were able to personally see the Messiah, the light of the world. Discuss with students how they decided which characteristics to describe. Are there common features among your students' answers?
5. Despite the centuries of waiting, there were believers of God who trusted that God would continue to be faithful and follow through on his promise to send the Savior. What does faithfulness look like for teenagers today? What areas of faithfulness did your students identify?

CLOSE

Remind students of Simeon and Anna's great commitment to God in spite of years of waiting for God to reveal himself. When that day came, Simeon said he could now die in peace. Have students bow their heads and then read Lamentations 3:22-24, a portion of Scripture that would've been familiar to Simeon and Anna. Close by reminding your students that God is faithful and has shown his faithfulness throughout history—and wants us to also be faithful as we develop godly character.

MORE

• **You can enrich this meeting by bringing in two older people from your church or neighborhood who have godly character and relate well to youth. Have them share examples from their lives when they had to work at being faithful to and trusting God. You may want to meet ahead of time with them, talk about what they could say, and let them know how much time they have to share. These can be powerful moments and models for the high schoolers.**

1. What are your family's traditions and customs? You know…little things you do regularly (sayings, trips, gifts, habits, routines) because, well, you've always done them. Write down two or three:

THE 12-YEAR-OLD TEACHER
Jesus visits the temple
(Luke 2:41-52)

2. What is a 12-year-old capable of doing? Put a "Y" next to the items you think a 12-year-old should be able or allowed to do, and an "N" next to ones that you think a 12-year-old can't or shouldn't do.

_____ Drive a car	_____ Have a cell phone
_____ Stay up past 10 p.m.	_____ Teach a lesson
_____ Talk with adults	_____ Lift weights
_____ Go on a date	_____ Solve an argument for others
_____ Think of others first	_____ Be helpful to parents
_____ Parachute out of a plane	_____ Drink coffee
_____ Go to PG-13 rated movies	_____ Love going to church

3. On what did Jesus focus in this story?

What do you think he was discussing with the teachers?

4. Which of the following best describes Jesus' response to his parents?

_____ I'm God's son, and I want to talk about God's Word.

_____ I'm safe and okay, just where I want to be—in God's house.

_____ You need to remember who my true Father is.

5. Read verses 51 and 52 and write down five things Jesus did as he grew up.

4. THE 12-YEAR-OLD TEACHER—Jesus visits the temple (Luke 2:41-52)

THIS WEEK

One of the few glimpses we get into Jesus' life as a young person is the remarkable account of him captivating the religious teachers in the temple court. Jesus was gone from his parents for a day before they noticed—and two more days before he was found. This lesson focuses on the growth of Jesus as a person and his knowledge of his mission.

OPENER

Divide your group into smaller teams of four to five people. Have everyone in each team share a story of an experience when they remember being really lost. Then ask for a few really lost stories that can be shared with the larger group. Keep it moving, but get two or three good ones. Now have team members share within the team a time when they remember surprising a parent, teacher, or coach by doing something really well as a kid. Again, after the teams have completed this exercise (three minutes or so), have each team offer its best example. Get two or three good ones before moving on. When this is finished, transition into the TalkSheet time by telling students you're going to look at a time in Jesus' childhood when he surprised the Jewish teachers and went missing from his parents for a few days.

DISCUSSION

1. Mary and Joseph went to Jerusalem not because it was a family tradition, but because they were participating in a religious custom required of every Israelite family: Attending Passover in Jerusalem (Deuteronomy 16:6). Beyond attending church and youth group, what are the major religious traditions for Christians? Should Christians have more religious traditions?

2. Ask your students how they decided which activities were possible and which weren't. List these reasons on a whiteboard as students tell you their answers. Some activities are dependent on laws (e.g., driving) or adults (e.g., movies or cell phones), but some of the answers will center on capabilities. After about two minutes of answers, have someone read Luke 2:41-52.

3. Jewish families in that culture and time often traveled in groups, or caravans, with many families together. In such a large group, it would've been easy for Mary and Joseph not to notice for a day that Jesus was gone. Jesus seems to have intentionally stayed behind to talk with the teachers of the law at the temple. Jesus was most likely discussing the Old Testament with the teachers. Can a 12-year-old understand the Bible? The Old Testament? Give your students a chance to talk about their answers here.

4. The response of Jesus to his parents shows that, though he grew in stages similar to other 12-year-olds, he was aware of his mission and his relationship to the Father. Ask students why they think his parents didn't seem to understand his character or role.

5. Luke is careful to point out after verse 49 that Jesus was obedient and that he grew in four distinct ways. Verse 52 is all that's written in Scripture of Jesus' life between age 12 and age 30. Have students look over their areas and give themselves a grade next to each, assessing their own growth. If appropriate, ask them to share how they determined their own grade.

CLOSE

This Scripture pictures Jesus as young, yet deeply committed to God's Word and the Father. Ask students to think about a scenario, but not share out loud: If they were to sit down with a teacher of the Bible and have a conversation, what would his or her response be? After a few moments, remind students that one great Christian tradition is to read and study the Bible. Ask students to share ways a commitment to know and understand God's Word will help them grow in "favor with God." Read Psalm 119:105 (NIV), "Your word is a lamp to my feet, and a light for my path," and ask students to look over their answers to #5 and consider how the Bible can be a guide to them in these areas.

MORE

Before the lesson, draw a pie-chart circle on a sheet of paper and divide it into four equal slices. Label one "my relationships," another "my mind," a third "my body," and a fourth "God." You can add some clip art, too— just make sure there's room in each quadrant for students to write a few sentences. Give a copy to each student and have them reflect on how they're doing at growing in each of these life areas—areas based on Luke 2:52. Have them list the people, activities, and groups in each area (background music works well for this type of activity). What's going well and what isn't in each of these areas? Which area looks like it needs some work? Are there some areas where not much is going on? What steps can we take to grow in neglected areas?

1. Write a short description of what temptation is and provide a real-life example:

2. Read through Matthew 4:1-11. Describe the three temptations Jesus faced in your own words:

1)

2)

3)

3. Put an X next to the three most common temptations that teenagers you know regularly face:

____ Cheating	____ Lying	____ Being proud
____ Drugs	____ Drinking	____ Being jealous
____ Being too sexual	____ Lusting	____ Giving up on commitments
____ Wasting time	____ Money	____ Eating

4. When you're facing temptations, where on the following scale would you place yourself?

◀ • ▶

I give in	I'm	I resist
easily	average	easily

5. The Bible says Jesus was tempted in every way, yet without sin (Hebrews 4:15). Jesus was tempted to fulfill his appetite, to be selfish, and to have immediate power and glory. These were all his to have, but were to be satisfied by the power of God the Father.

a. What is one temptation that you are facing right now?

b. Which, if any, of the three temptations (appetite, selfish gain, or power) is your temptation most like?

c. Check any of the following that will be your next step in dealing with this:

____ Find a trusted Christian friend or adult and ask them to help me deal with this.

____ Pray about it.

____ Flee from it—don't put myself in a position to be tempted again.

____ Read sections from the Bible that deal with this area and remind me of who God is.

THIS WEEK

Adolescents face a variety of temptations, many for the first time—and with considerable social pressures. Immediately after Jesus was baptized, he was led to the wilderness where he experienced significant temptation. This TalkSheet focuses on Christ's temptations and connects them to the struggles and temptations students face.

OPENER

Announce that today you'll discuss the very popular topic of temptation, and you want to do an informal survey of the group. Post five large signs around the room—or have volunteers hold them up—that detail some temptations we have to deal with on a regular basis. You'll want to keep this opening lighthearted, so pick five items like chocolate or candy, computer or video game time, sarcasm, putting off homework, and procrastination. Ask each group member to go to the sign that represents their biggest temptation. Once the students are in place, ask students in each group to share with others why that temptation is their biggest. To expand this exercise, ask each group to create an advertising slogan demonstrating why that particular temptation is so appealing. Allow no more than five minutes for this task, then ask a representative of each group to present the slogan.

Have the students return to their seats and ask them to list some common temptations (real ones) they see friends and others struggling with regularly. List their answers on a whiteboard. If you're unsure about an answer, or about whether it's common, check for clarification with them or other students in the group, but don't appear to question the truthfulness of the answer—affirm the student's answer before checking.

DISCUSSION

1. Students know what temptation is, but different people describe it differently. Have a handful of students share their definitions. Point out the variety of perspectives among students. You may want to ask what a spiritual temptation would look like.
2. It may be helpful to perform a melodrama at this point, with the leader reading the story while two students or adult leaders act it out up front. As the leader reads, the actors perform the actions and repeat the quotes after they're read. Make sure to pick two actors who will give it extra energy!
3. In Luke 4:13, the Bible says that the devil had finished "every temptation." These three tests of appetite, selfish gain, and power are temptations students face today. Make three columns on the whiteboard with these as the column headings. Have students give examples of *specific* temptations that teenagers face that fall in one or more of these categories.
4. It's important to affirm students in this section. It'll be easy for them to feel as if they're not measuring up. You may want students to review their self-ranking and ask if they're being too easy or tough on themselves.
5. Students need to not only know about temptation, but also to recognize areas of temptation in their own lives and take action. This exercise will help and may be difficult for some students. As students complete these, you may want to ask for a show of hands to find out how many were able to identify something in question 5b. Note that in most instances, you should check all four blanks in question 5c.

CLOSE

Some have noted that the temptations of Genesis 3:1, 4, and 5 are also of appetite, selfishness, and power. It might be helpful to show these verses to students and remind them that often our temptations are to satisfy an appetite (which isn't just food), to be self-serving, or to gain significance. Allow students a moment of silent prayer, letting them focus on praying about their answers to question 5.

MORE

• **One of the great temptations is to *do* something that we think will improve who we are. We want people to admire or appreciate us for what we *do* versus seeing obedience as an act of love to God. You may want to have students reflect on this as it relates to their school or neighborhood.**
• **We'll give in to something so others like us even though these actions may go against who God wants us to be. There's an element of putting our trust in God, that his way is best, when we face temptation. Have students discuss ways that facing temptations confronts our hesitation to trust God. It may be helpful to discuss the concept of instant gratification from questions 1 and 3. How does giving in to temptation fulfill a short-term need while ignoring or destroying long-term wellbeing?**
• **You could close by conducting an exercise where students write down what regularly tempts them on 3 x 5 cards. You can then have them nail their temptations to a cross as a symbol of Christ's power over sin provided through his death and resurrection. What is your students' job from this point on regarding temptation?**

1. Make a list of the items you own, the activities you do, or the relationships you have that are the most important to you. Write as many as you can!

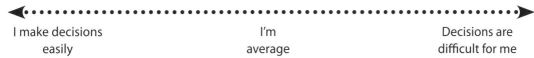

LEAVING THE NETS
The calling of the disciples
(Mark 1:14-20)

2. Read Mark 1:14-20. Rank yourself on the scale below on how good you are at making decisions.

◀ • ▶

I make decisions   I'm   Decisions are
easily   average   difficult for me

3. Jesus says that the kingdom will ask people to repent and believe. For each of these words, write a sentence that describes or gives an example of what those words look like. Look up Acts 2:38 and Romans 1:16 for additional help.

Repent:

Believe:

4. Each disciple in this story left his job in the family's business to follow Jesus. Parents and family can play a variety of roles in our spiritual lives. Put an X on each line below that best describes your situation.

◀ • ▶

My parents support   My parents don't
my Christian faith.   support my faith.

◀ • ▶

My parents model   My parents don't model
how to follow Christ.   how to follow Christ.

5. Write down two key ways you can follow Christ and let him lead you this next week.

THIS WEEK

An important part of the life of Christ was his relationship with his disciples, the people he invited to be with him daily and learn from him as he taught and healed. Today many people describe a Christian the same way—one who follows after Christ. This scene is the first of many in the life of Christ where he calls people to follow him because God's kingdom has come to earth, and it provides an introduction to the biblical theme of discipleship.

OPENER

Think through some of your favorite movies with scenes depicting following—when people serve as accomplices or apprentices and learn from leaders. If appropriate for your group, show this scene and then ask students to identify ways in which the follower is learning from the leader. Ask students for other movie examples where someone was following and learning from a master. You can list these on the board and, when finished, ask students to compare that list with the way the biblical disciples learned from Jesus. Let students make comments and list these on the board as well.

Ask students if they've ever been to a really great concert. Ask some of them to describe what it was like to anticipate the moment when the band came onstage. What did the crowd do? Take as many of these answers as you can, but keep it moving along.

Today's story is the moment in Christ's life where Jesus declares God has come on the scene in human form and the rules will change. No longer will living be just about obedience, but about forgiveness through repentance, and about God's grace to those who follow his Son.

DISCUSSION

1. Ask students to imagine that Jesus asked them to lay these down and follow him. Have students circle the most difficult two or three on the list. Ask for reasons why these would be difficult. This is similar to what the disciples did when they left their jobs as fishermen and their family business. That took a lot of trust. Why did the disciples trust Jesus so easily?
2. Some make decisions quickly, while others wrestle with choices. Ask students how they determined where to rank themselves on this line. Jesus was declaring that God's kingdom had come, and he invited his listeners to enter that kingdom. How do students make decisions?

3. Ask students to share a definition they think is particularly good. *Repent* means to change one's life based on a new understanding of life, sin, and righteousness. *Believe* means more than just knowing about God (James 2:19). It implies a level of trust that places us in God's care. We can trust Jesus, who calls himself the Good Shepherd (John 10:11, 14).
4. Tell students that *follow* literally means to "follow behind" the master. Simon and Andrew still had contact with their family (verses 29, 30) and James and John were not poor, as their business had hired servants (verse 20). Rather, following Jesus meant trusting him by changing their vocation from businessmen to Christ-followers—a choice that would lead to persecution and, for some, execution for their faith in Christ and preaching the gospel. Ask students what role their parent(s) play in their Christian faith.
5. Prompt students to think about two action steps they can take to follow Christ this next week. Maybe it's a new habit at home, or with friends, or spending time with God in prayer, or learning more about God through reading the Bible.

CLOSE

The call of Christ is for people to follow him, trusting that he is the Good Shepherd and has our best interests in mind. Sometimes Jesus asks his followers to leave behind their nets, their goods, and even more to follow him. How are you doing at following Christ? When do you say, "I'll follow you, just as long as I can keep _____"? Close in prayer and allow students to pray about their answers to question 5.

MORE

• The popular old game of Simon Says works well with this lesson because it connects with following someone. If your group size or setting allows it, a creative edition of Follow the Leader around your building or outdoors might work, too. You could also do a blindfolded trust walk where students pair up and take turns being blindfolded and led around by the teammate.

• The trust issue is a significant one. When faced with social pressures, academic pressures, family pressures, and expectations from others (like coaches or directors), it's difficult to know how to make decisions. You may want to explore the issue of trust in your students' lives. Verses on trust you can give students to look up include Psalm 37:3 and 56:11; Isaiah 12:2; and 1 Timothy 6:17.

1. Which of the following is the best description of what "the best" means?

_____ Superior to others

_____ Consistent in quality

_____ Outperforms

_____ Exceeds expectations

_____ Makes me and others happy

_____ Comforting

_____ Changes how I think about it

_____ Is revolutionary and new

WATER INTO WINE
The first miracle at Cana
(John 2:1-11)

2. Jesus transformed water into wine. What does transformation mean?

3. Get in groups of three or more and pick two of the following passages: 2 Corinthians 5:16-19; Ephesians 2:8-9; or Colossians 3:5-10. Write down any phrases or ideas that best fit under each of these headings.

Old Way Before Christ	What Christ Does	New Way After Christ

4. What Jesus made was considered the best. List three ways a Christian can demonstrate the best of who God is in the world.

5. Look over the following areas and check the ones where you've seen God help you change.

____ Relationship with parents	____ Obeying	____ Future vocation
____ Worship	____ Language	____ Study habits
____ Ability to be myself	____ Dealing with problems	____ Care for friends
____ It's difficult to see changes	____ Temper	____ Worry
____ Other ways	____ Thought life	____ Love

THIS WEEK

The first miracle of Jesus took place in what would be a familiar setting—the middle of a crowd. While attending the wedding of someone who probably either knew Mary or Nathaniel (John 21:2), Mary displayed her understanding of who Jesus was by asking him to fix a serious social problem for the wedding hosts. Jesus took the unclean (stone jars of water) and made something new and of the best quality; he can do the same thing in our lives. This TalkSheet provides ample opportunity for you and your students to discuss this.

OPENER

Set up four tables around your room ahead of time and have the ultimate taste test of sodas. The cola wars are intense advertising battles, and every student has a favorites, so hype this opening activity before starting it. Set up four tables. On each table, put small sample cups of cola (1), root beer (2), clear soda (3), and some other type of soda (4). Set out as many cups as you have students for each type of drink on each table, making sure to label each cup Type 1, 2, 3, or 4.

Give each student a sheet of paper with four columns labeled "Cola," "Root Beer," "Clear," and "Other," and tell them to go around to the four tables and do taste tests. At each table they're to identify each type of drink and write it down, marking a star next to the one they like best at each table.

If your group is too big for this activity, do it up front and select just three people to come up and compete. After the activity, read off the answers and survey which sodas the students liked best at each table.

DISCUSSION

1. Students may say they want to pick more than one, but have them choose only one. Once everyone has finished, lead a quick discussion on why they chose the one they did. After a few minutes, ask the group how they determined which of the answers to pick—which one was best. Jesus' first miracle reveals that he was interested in helping create something new in people, something that was the best. Read John 2:1-11.

2. Allow some students to share their definitions and write some of the key phrases on the board. Transfor-

mation involves an act of changing one thing into another, the new being something with a different composition. Some might call it *conversion*. Ask students whether something can transform itself or whether transformation comes from an outside source.

3. These are substantial passages to discuss—it'll take some time to work through. Make two columns on a whiteboard and allow students to voice their answers. Keep in mind the idea of transformation: What role does Christ play in this transformation process? What's our responsibility in this transformation?

4. Some people see being a Christian as a life of dos and don'ts as opposed to living the best life. Students' answers may focus on key words like faith, love, hope, or holiness. Do your students have a good idea of how a Christian demonstrates God's best?

5. It's a good practice to stop and look at what God has done in our lives. Tell students it's okay if they can't easily identify anything here. Remind students of God's love for them and that he wants to do a work in their lives to make them the best of his creation.

CLOSE

Read verse 11 and tell students that this first miracle illustrates both what God can do in our lives and why he does it. He wants to transform us so that people see our lives and see God's best in action— so God gets the glory and people learn to put their faith in Jesus Christ. Have students look over their responses to question 5 and think of ways their lives can reflect the best for God this week. After a few moments for silent reflection and personal prayer, close with prayer.

MORE

One of the symbolic elements to this story was the role and use of the stone jars. Stone jars were very common and were considered ceremonially unclean by the teachers of the day. A considerable controversy of the day involved ceremonial washing before eating (Mark 7:1-5), a traditional ritual not mandated by Scripture. Jesus took the elements of an artificial ritual over which people judged others, and performed a miracle of grace that illustrated a better way. Think of rituals we perform today that God may want to use to show grace to others rather than have them used as measuring sticks by which to judge others.

1. In a typical week in your life, how often do you get angry? Place yourself on the scale below:

Hardly get angry at all

About once a day

A few times a day

I am regularly angry

JESUS AND ANGER
The temple is cleansed
(John 2:13-17)

How would you finish this statement? When I get angry, it's usually because—

2. Check out Mark 3:1-6. What does Jesus get angry about in this story?

Now read Mark 10:13-16. Who is Jesus upset with here and why?

3. Read Ephesians 4:26-27 and answer the following questions:
Is it okay to get angry? Why?

What should a Christian be quick to do when he or she is angry?

What's the danger in staying angry for a long time?

4. Next to each of the following, put "A" if you agree and "D" if you disagree with the statement.
____ A person should never admit to being angry.
____ Anger is best handled by ignoring it or keeping it inside.
____ Angry feelings usually go away if you don't deal with them.
____ Anger is best expressed freely and quickly.
____ Anger is a part of life, but forgiveness must quickly follow.

5. How can we learn to handle anger effectively?

THIS WEEK

Anger and adolescence seem to go hand-in-hand. Everyone experiences anger, and it's not always wrong to be angry. Yet anger is considered a leading cause of many other problems that plague people. This scene in the life of Christ provides a rich opportunity to discuss when and why Jesus got angry and to examine other verses that deal with anger. Students will compare when and why they get angry in light of Christ's example.

OPENER

Welcome students to a Pet Peeve Support Group where they can support each other as they put up with little things that annoy them in life. Have students team up with one or two others and share their top two pet peeves. After three or four minutes, ask teams to share some examples of unusual pet peeves. Have fun with this one and encourage lots of laughter (without pointing at specific students). Let students share their pet peeves freely, and ask students to clarify or explain why they have a particular pet peeve. You'll want to prep a good story about your own "best" pet peeve to close this out. Transition into the discussion by working on a group definition of *pet peeve* and writing it on the board. When finished, tell students that today's story focuses on a moment when Jesus got angry, which will provide a chance for them to look at anger.

DISCUSSION

1. This first question moves past pet peeves to anger. Ask students what they noticed about themselves and anger. Was it easy or difficult to be honest about getting angry? In reality, people usually get angry when they feel unaccepted, ignored, controlled, or interested only in themselves. If it's difficult for students to share out loud about anger, keep moving by reading John 2:13-17. What was Jesus upset about in this story? How do you know Jesus was upset? The people were selling animals for sacrifices and exchanging money for pilgrims who needed to pay the temple tax. It no doubt became more than a ministry for the pilgrims and developed into a business producing significant profits.

2. Do you notice a pattern in when Jesus gets angry and at whom? Jesus gets angry with people who are religious, but who don't have a love for God and keep others from experiencing God's love. But what was Jesus' response to the sinners around him?

3. The subject of anger can stimulate a lively discussion—there are many opinions about it. The Bible uses different Greek words to describe anger. This passage acknowledges that people can get angry and not sin. The key is to only be angry about what God gets angry about—and that's the problem. We usually get angry for selfish reasons. When that happens, we need to deal with it as this passage indicates—by settling our anger quickly with forgiveness and not letting it become wrath. It can develop into bitterness and sin, which can produce long-term spiritual trouble and create a foothold for the devil to create significant problems in our lives.

4. Go through each statement and ask students to raise their hands to indicate their answer. The first four are incorrect statements about anger, yet they're common ways people deal with anger. If these are incorrect, how did we learn to handle anger in these ways?

5. What role does forgiveness play in dealing with anger? Is it easier to ask for forgiveness or give forgiveness? Are there people with whom you're still angry where forgiveness is needed?

CLOSE

Read James 1:19-20 and tell students that, though anger is part of being human, we're told to be "slow to anger"—to not be easily angered or provoked. Most people get angry about issues that are quite different from the things that angered Jesus. Remind students of Jesus' model for us and his invitation to follow him. Remind them that while he hung on the cross, even then he modeled a life of forgiveness and grace.

MORE

• **If you want to help your students work on anger, writer and therapist Les Parrot (in *Helping the Struggling Adolescent*) suggests having students compose a "hassle log" for a week where they record the moments when they get upset. The columns can note the place, what happened, the person/people, what they said/didn't say, and the student's response. A great addition would be to have the bottom half of the sheet be a "blessing log" where students record moments when they were blessed. This helps them see not only where things go wrong for them, but also where things go well.**

• **Moments of anger can be very revealing for high school students if they analyze why they're getting angry. Many students will find that they're fighting to get something—peace, recognition, acceptance, or other things they desire. Others may discover that they're really mad at themselves (though it may not initially look like that) and they really don't like who they are. Both are worth exploring and talking about to a trusted adult at church. Some students have deep-rooted anger issues from earlier in life. In these cases, professional Christian counseling may be needed.**

1. What do you think are the most common misconceptions people have about Christianity? Check the top reason.

____ It's about following rules.

____ People are Christian because their parents are.

____ Everybody is already a Christian.

____ Jesus is just one way to get to God.

____ You have to be sad to be a Christian.

____ You have to like potluck dinners.

____ Other _____.

MIDNIGHT MEETING
Nicodemus visits Jesus
(John 3:1-21; 7:50-51; 19:38-40)

2. Nicodemus came to Jesus in the middle of the night. Why do you think this religious leader did that? Check as many answers as you want.

____ It was the only time he was free since he worked in the daytime.

____ He was afraid of being seen by the other religious leaders.

____ It symbolizes his own spiritual darkness.

____ He wanted to have an uninterrupted time to talk.

____ He wanted to have a private conversation with Jesus.

3. Read John 3:14-18 and then answer the following:

How is salvation like getting a new start?

What do the following verses say about what Jesus did?
Verse 14:

Verse 16:

What does verse 17 say about why Christ came into the world?

4. Read John 7:50-51 and 19:38-40. What did Nicodemus do?

5. Is your Christian faith a secret from your friends and those who know you?

If you were meeting with Jesus face-to-face, what would you talk about?

THIS WEEK

We live in a time where spirituality and religion are prominent topics on the Internet, television, and in our culture. Even those who aren't religious bring up the topic. The story of Nicodemus shows how people who saw Jesus' ministry and miracles wanted to know more about him. This TalkSheet helps students to learn more about Nicodemus' nighttime visit and to discuss the topic of salvation.

OPENER

Some people enjoy being up at night, while others like to be active during the daytime. Light and dark are key parts of the story of Nicodemus' visiting Jesus. Designate one side of the room "daytime" and the other "nighttime." Ask students to move to one side or the other based on which they prefer. Now announce there's a third time of day most teenagers don't prefer, but ask those who like to be up in the mornings to move to the back of the room. Few, if any, students will move there, but once everyone has decided, ask for some reasons why they made the choice they did. After a few minutes, tell students that today's story takes place at night—an important illustration for John, the writer, as he tells the story of Nicodemus, who moves from spiritual darkness into the light of following Christ. Have students return to their seats.

DISCUSSION

1. Many misconceptions exist regarding Christianity. Much of the confusion comes from words Christians use. Have a student read John 3:1-8. Ask students which they think best describes what it means to become a Christian—to be "born again" or to be "born from above"? Why? Ask students if they think people perceive a negative meaning in the phrase "born again."

2. All these answers are held by scholars as possible reasons why Nicodemus came to Jesus that night. No one knows for certain, but the night meeting does serve as a symbol for John later in the passage. In the book of John, Jesus is shown as the light of the world (John 8:12) and those who don't believe in him are described as being in spiritual darkness (3:19-22). Do you think there's more evil in the nighttime than in the daytime? Do people act differently at night than in the daytime?

3. You'll get a variety of answers; ask students to share what they wrote. Point out that God gives us a new start and a new nature. When we put our faith in Christ, we're not only forgiven of the past, but also given a new nature powered by the Holy Spirit (2 Corinthians 5:17). Remind students that Jesus came into the world to save the world because of God's great love and that there's a judgment for those who don't believe. Still, Jesus' desire is that people put their faith in him (John 5:24).

4. Let students share their observations on the verses. Nicodemus defended Jesus in front of the other Pharisees and then was ridiculed for it. He also aided in the burial of Jesus, bringing a generous amount of burial spices—also at night. Ask students whether they think people knew Nicodemus was a follower of Christ or whether he was a secret disciple.

5. Ask your students to reflect on their answers. Many times we may have a strong faith, but we don't let our friends know about that. They may know we're religious, but we're careful in how we talk and what we talk about with them. The last question may be a good one to talk through and discover your students' uncertainty about a variety of topics.

CLOSE

This is a great lesson for challenging your students about their own relationship with Christ. Nicodemus gives an example of a secret follower, one who still has questions about Jesus and his teaching. Pass out reaction cards to students so they can respond to the lesson. You may want to play a song as they fill them out. The cards can have a place for their name and contact info, and then you can think of two or three quick questions.

MORE

• One of the issues this passage can raise is that of baptism. Though various churches practice it differently, baptism is a central practice for Christians (Matthew 28:18-20 and Acts 2:41). Jesus' use of the word "water" in verse 5 has been interpreted differently. It was used in a way Nicodemus could understand, so it either referred to John the Baptist's ministry (Matthew 3:1-6) or the Old Testament's teaching regarding the cleansing power of the Spirit of God (Ezekiel 36:24-27). The latter seems to fit better with other parts of the New Testament that show a connection between water and the Spirit (Titus 3:5).

1. Are there certain types of people who annoy you or seem difficult to get to know? Maybe when you first meet them suspicious or negative thoughts go through your head. Which of the following types of people are like that for you? Check the three most difficult types for you.

____ Bossy people

____ Quiet people

____ People who are tall or short

____ Older people

____ Talkative people

____ People who look poor

____ People of different ethnicity

____ Musical people

____ Good athletes

____ Smart people

____ Lazy people

____ Popular people

____ Dirty people

____ People who have the "look" that you'd like to have

____ Other _____

2. Think of the students at your school everyone either ignores or picks on. A traditional term for these people is "social outcasts." Team up with two or three others and come up with a good description of what it means to be a social outcast, based on what you've observed.

3. Compare John 4:10 and 14 with John 7:37-39.
Why did Jesus talk about "living water?"

How does "living water" help describe what it means to be a Christian?

4. Look over John 4:10-15 again. Why didn't Jesus just tell her who he was?

5. In light of Jesus' example, what three steps can you take this week to help those around you who may be outcast or need a better understanding of God to satisfy their spiritual thirst?

THIS WEEK

The story of Jesus' encounter with the woman at the well is one of the more familiar ones from the Bible. A great account of how Christ came for all, it has often been used as a model for relational evangelism. Another key theme from the story centers on Jesus' intentional crossing of social, ethnic, and religious barriers. This lesson focuses students' attention on this aspect of the story and leads them to think about barriers in their lives that may need to be crossed in their efforts to live as an example and encouragement to others.

OPENER

Tell students that today's story focuses on a scene where Jesus crossed significant social barriers to minister to a woman. Every society struggles with people who are different from each other working to get along. Ask students to list for you all such barriers they can think of in our society. Write each on the board. You should have a long list, but you may need to prompt them to think of racial, gender, social, physical, and religious examples.

Jesus, in this story, meets a Samaritan woman. She was very different from Nicodemus, who was in a highly respected position; this woman was despised by many for a variety of reasons. Prearrange with three students (one guy, one girl, one narrator) to read this passage as a drama, each taking the appropriate part. Have them practice it beforehand with an adult coach so it's done well.

DISCUSSION

1. Ask them to look over their answers and to share what qualities they observe about their three choices that bother them the most—what barriers from the opener separate *them* from others?

2. Have groups quickly share their responses. Ask them how they feel when they see this happening and let them share a bit. Then gently (gently!) remind them that some of them sometimes treat others that way as well. We may or may not be aware of it, but we're like the disciples in this story in trying to avoid certain people or, worse, treating them poorly. Samaritans were part Jew and part Gentile, and they had their own religious system of worship that didn't center on Jerusalem. The Jews despised them as outcasts. In fact, Jesus was mocked by being called a Samaritan in John 8:48.

3. Ask for student responses. Some will point to Jesus' wanting to use an object lesson, since they were at a well. There are some Scriptures that support Jesus' use of water here, the best known being Jeremiah 2:13. The Bible also says that turning from sin and believing in Christ can lead to being "refreshed" (Acts 3:19). Ask students what that word means to them and whether it describes their relationship with God. If they don't like it, listen for other words that may work better.

4. This gives you a chance to talk about being a witness to others. Do your students talk to others about their relationship with Christ? Do they pray for opportunities to be a witness? Do they invite others to come with them to your group? These are key practices for students who want to be a witness to others.

5. Hopefully you've created an atmosphere in which students can answer this question truthfully and sensitively. You want students to push themselves here and see their behaviors toward others with great self-awareness.

CLOSE

The story begins, "Now he had to go through Samaria" (verse 4). Most Jews avoided this route through Samaria and crossed the Jordan River to avoid the Samaritan people. So why did Jesus decide to go through Samaria? Jesus had an appointment with a Samaritan woman that was important for his disciples (verse 27) and that village (verses 39-42) to see. The early ministry of the church was to include the Samaritans (Acts 1:8; 8:48). So what are the areas that we may "have" to go through to be obedient to God? Close with prayer, asking that your group would follow Christ's example and have the courage to follow the steps they've written down for the last question.

MORE

• **When we read stories like this we don't always understand the emotional level of the racist views in it. This is a great lesson to challenge you and your group about modern-day social barriers, particularly those of racism and social class. Most youth groups are pretty homogeneous in nature—the students come from similar backgrounds. The following are some great resources on teens and racism.**
About.com "Teaching Teenagers About Prejudice"
The Skin We're In: Teaching Our Teens to Be Emotionally Strong, Socially Smart, and Spiritually Connected
Hate Hurts: How Children Learn and Unlearn Prejudice, a joint project by the Anti-Defamation League, Barnes & Noble, and Scholastic Publishing
"Take the Pledge to Stop Hate"—goes with *Hate Hurts*

1. Describe your hometown (city, town, area) in three words.

HOMETOWN PROPHET
Jesus rejected by those who knew him the longest
(Luke 4:16-30)

2. Team up with two others and read Mark 6:1-6. How would you describe people's reaction to Jesus as he stood up and read?

Read verse 28. When has a group of people been angry with you? What was it about?

3. Rewrite the following phrases from the passage in Mark so that others can understand what Jesus said he'd come to do.

"God has anointed me" -

"Proclaim good news to the poor" -

"Proclaim freedom to the prisoners" -

"Give sight to the blind" -

"Set the oppressed free" -

"Proclaim the year of the Lord's favor" -

4. How well does your youth group ministry do in these areas? Rate your group for each of the following items on a scale of 1 to 5, with 5 being the highest.

Helping the poor/needy _____   Seeing people set free _____

Helping students deal with problems_____   Proclaiming God's salvation _____

5. Consider this: Byron is deeply committed to Jesus and wants to obey God. Yet he often feels misunderstood by teachers, adults, and others who don't understand his faith. Even his friends from church aren't very supportive at times. Team up with two or three others and discuss what two pieces of advice you'd give Byron to stay strong in this area. Write your group's answers below:

THIS WEEK

This TalkSheet focuses on one of the most dramatic moments in Jesus' early ministry. The significance of it may be lost on readers today, but for the people who were actually there it was an incredible moment. Jesus had lived with them for almost 30 years as a carpenter's son, but on this day he stood up to read from the prophets and then claimed he fulfilled the prophecy of the Messiah. This TalkSheet will teach students about Jesus' ministry and lead them to think about the quality of their own youth group's ministry.

OPENER

Divide your group into equal teams of six to 10 students and tell them you're going to host a fabulous game show called *Guess Where They Are!* Get your students clapping as if they're a game show audience—an "applause" sign might help. Before the meeting, go around your area and take 20 or more digital pictures of different spots. Pick the best 10 and use a presentation program to create a slide show. Give each team a sheet of paper with numbers 1 through 10 on it and tell students to write down where the picture was taken. (You can see you'll want to be creative with your picture-taking and also have various levels of difficulty.) After you show the 10 shots, go back through them and give the answers. Have teams check off the number they got correct. The team with the highest score gets a prize.

Today's TalkSheet focuses on a key scene in Jesus' early ministry—his dramatic Scripture reading in the synagogue of his hometown, Nazareth. In that scene, the townspeople respond in anger and almost kill Jesus—but the scene also shows us what Jesus' ministry was about and why hurting and outcast people loved him. Have someone read Luke 4:16-30.

DISCUSSION

1. Have students quickly share their words with you. There'll be some funny ones and unusual ones. Feel free to ask for further reasons and examples as you go. This needs to be an upbeat sharing time for your whole group, so keep it fast-paced and draw out some students who may not normally share.

2. Make sure students share their answers with others within their group. Have a few of the students share their memories of those angry moments. Why did they pick the moment they picked? How do you think Jesus felt about the people's anger? Ask students to consider Jesus' response in Luke 23:33-34.

3. The passage Jesus read is from Isaiah 61:1, 2. This question will take some time to complete, and students may not be able to think of examples for every one. That's okay, but you may want to help them think. While each is literally true, it could also mean something spiritually. The "year of the Lord's favor" (verse 7) is a reference to the Jubilee year. Every 50 years, property was returned and slaves were freed (see Leviticus 25:8-55 for more background info), and this was called Jubilee. It was an illustration of God's power

to save the Israelite people. In reading the Isaiah Scripture, Jesus was clearly letting his listeners know that he was the One who would ultimately fulfill God's salvation plan.

4. Don't be afraid to allow students to evaluate your youth ministry group in these four areas. It'll raise some good issues focusing on how your youth ministry helps students. Ask students how the group does in these areas. Figure out the average score for each (if your group is small) or allow students to give you feedback in general. Is it important that we're good at these areas? Why or why not? What would a better job look like in these areas?

5. This question is open-ended on purpose—it'll give you a chance to hear a variety of responses from your students. What was the role of the church youth group in Byron's situation? Ask your students if any of them ever feel like that. *Should we start with each other as we decide what to discuss today? What would that take?*

CLOSE

Pass out 3 x 5 cards for students to write on. Read Luke 4:18-19, then tell students Jesus came to help those in need, to free people from oppression, and to offer salvation to the world. As they hear that, is their first thought "I want to do that" or is it "I really need that in my life"? Either answer is okay— many of us feel both in a given year. Tell students to put their name and contact info on the card and then write down their response to these questions:

1. Where do you feel you need to experience God's ministry in your life?
2. How do you want to help others through this youth ministry and in what ways?

Tell students the cards will only be seen by the adult leaders in the group. Collect the cards and pray with students.

MORE

• **This Bible story is shown on the DVD *Jesus of Nazareth*. The movie adds features, but the general message is still present. Use it to set the tone for the significance of Jesus' words—how people knew he meant he was the Messiah. You can also find a clip from the movie online on YouTube.com.**

• **Jesus gives two examples (verses 25-27) of God blessing Sidon and Syria, two towns considered heathen and full of Gentiles. So when God blessed those towns and not Nazareth (verse 24), the crowd reacted in anger because of their racism and spiritual selfishness. We need to be aware of our own potential to react similarly. Are there neighborhoods or people in your hometown to whom you think God would never send blessings? What parts of town do people you know talk poorly about? What lessons from this story can we learn and put into action in our own lives?**

1. Think of the best picture ever taken of you. Share with a few people around you why it was the best. What quality of you did it capture that you liked?

Team up with one or two others and, for each of the following snapshots, read the verses and answer the snapshot question in each frame.

---

2. James and John (nicknamed by Jesus "sons of thunder," Mark 3:17)
Read: Mark 10:35-37, 41; Luke 9:54.
What were the two desires in these two stories?

How might this connect to being called "sons of thunder"?

---

3. Andrew
Read: John 1:40-42; 6:8-9; 12:21-23
What is Andrew doing in each of these three stories?

If Andrew was at your school or in your youth group, what might he spend time doing with his friends?

---

4. Nathanael
Read: John 1:45-49
What kind of response did Nathanael give Philip?

How did Jesus deal with Nathanael?

---

5. Thomas (also called Didymus)
Read: John 20:20-28
Why did Thomas doubt?
What was his response after seeing Jesus?

Read: John 11:14-16 and 14:5-6.
What kinds of personality traits are seen here? How might those contribute to doubt?

---

6. Which of the four snapshots is most like you? Why? How has your personality helped you in your faith, or has it been hard to deal with?

THIS WEEK

The 12 who followed Jesus were the main focus of his discipleship ministry. Invited to follow him, the 12 disciples came from a variety of backgrounds and eventually launched the church after Pentecost. This TalkSheet introduces students to the disciples and, through focusing on five of them, helps students identify with some of the issues they present.

OPENER

Give everyone a 3 x 5 card and ask them to write their name at the top of the card. Then have them write any of their nicknames below. Make sure they write legibly! Then collect the cards, look for interesting ones, and see if the students can guess who has that nickname. You may want to ask students how they got a certain nickname. Did anyone get one because of their personality or how they act? Do any of them have a nickname based on a physical feature (hair, height, and so on)?

DISCUSSION

1. Ask students how they determined which picture was their best. Write their answers on the left side of the whiteboard. Then ask students to report *why* it was the best picture taken of them. Write those on the right side. Then ask, "Does a picture accurately capture who you are? Why or why not?" Tell students, "In the Bible we read a lot about the 12 disciples as a group, but don't know much about them individually. Today we're going to look at four snapshots of disciples who will help us consider our own relationship to Christ."

2. Before the resurrection and Pentecost, James and John didn't understand what kind of kingdom Jesus would be ruling. They wanted to be great and respected—things that might come from being a member of a wealthy family with servants (Mark 1:20). What kind of personality do these two have? James and John both wrote books that are part of the New Testament. James became the leader of the church in Jerusalem while John became a leading apostle of the church after Pentecost (Acts 8:14) and encouraged Paul and his ministry (Galatians 2:9). He was banished to the Island of Patmos where he had the visions that formed his writing of Revelation. Make two columns on the whiteboard, one featuring what James and John were like before Pentecost and one that listed what they did after Pentecost.

3. Each time we see Andrew, he's bringing someone to Jesus. Discuss that with your students. What kind of people did Andrew bring? Why did he bring them? In what ways was Andrew an encourager to others?

4. Most think Nathanael's nickname was Bartholomew because that's the name associated with a disciple in other passages of the Bible. Nathanael's sarcastic comment showed his disrespect of Nazareth and his limited view of what God could do. Once Jesus demonstrated his supernatural ability, Nathanael's response showed his knowledge of the Old Testament and his understanding of who Jesus was. Is it okay to be sarcastic? What effect does sarcasm have on someone's commitment to God?

5. Thomas' encounter with Christ shows his doubt—his lack of trust. Ask students, "What other personality traits did you notice about Thomas?" It's possible Thomas was a fearful and pessimistic person. How does fear contribute to doubt? Does pessimism weaken people's faith? Why or why not?

6. It's encouraging to see that the Bible is filled with normal, imperfect people who can show us God's power to transform us. Despite their struggles and hesitation, God used these disciples and others to spread the gospel and help start the church. It's easy to get discouraged about our faults, and sometimes it's difficult to think God can use us for something great. Let students discuss their ideas for ways their personalities affect their relationship with God.

CLOSE

It's important to remember that *God* is the one who transforms our lives. While we can do things to help in that process, like praying and reading the Bible, God is the only one who can take imperfect people and do great things. The disciples surrendered their lives to Christ and his direction. They were empowered by the Holy Spirit to go out and be dynamic witnesses to the world. Close with prayer for yourself and your students, asking that this same history of impact can be their own personal history.

MORE

Try creating "disciple snapshots" of your students beforehand. A week or two ahead of time, use a digital camera to take pictures of your students. Print each one on a 8.5 x 11 sheet so that each student has his or her own page. Create two columns under their photos, the first titled "What I'm like" and the other "What God is doing in my life." Pass these sheets out to the students to fill out themselves. After five minutes or so, allow everyone to walk around and add appropriate comments to the papers of others. Make sure that you write positive comments that reinforce the good things you see in each student. You may prefer to write a comment in each column on every student's sheet before that day to save time and influence others to write positive comments.

1. When have you experienced the most pain or discomfort due to an injury or illness?

BEING WHOLE AGAIN
Jesus' healings
(Luke 5:12-26)

2. Read Luke 5:12-13. Imagine you've been a leper and an outcast for a long time. What do you think it would've felt like to be a leper and finally have someone touch your skin?

3. Read Luke 5:17-26 again. Imagine you're creating a short movie about this story. What would be the most dramatic scene? Why?

How would you shoot it to best capture the emotional qualities of the scene?

4. Which of the following characters in the story are you most like? Circle one.

The Pharisees	The friends
The man on the mat	The crowd

Why did you select them?

5. Jesus first forgave the man before healing him. It's easy to create a wish list of things we'd like to change about ourselves physically—but if we were to create a list of spiritual changes, what are two or three you'd like?

_____ Have more faith	_____ Have certainty that God loves me
_____ Help others come to Jesus	_____ Read the Bible more
_____ Understand that Bible better	_____ Pray more
_____ Be a better example for others	_____ Be less fearful
_____ Know God's will for my life	_____ Really experience God's forgiveness
_____ Be less judgmental	_____ Other _____

THIS WEEK

One of the main aspects of Jesus' ministry was his miracles, many of which were healing the sick. These outward healings were a demonstration of Jesus' power over sickness and disease, and they served as a physical symbol of how Christ can make us whole in our souls. This TalkSheet looks at two men who came to Jesus in very different ways, but who both experienced his healing power.

OPENER

Divide your students into groups of no less than five or six. Have each group pick four members whom the others will safely and carefully lift up over their shoulders and back down again. Make sure one or two of the group serve as spotters while three or four can lift. On your "go," see which group can complete the task of lifting each person over shoulders and back down. Afterward, give the groups two or three minutes to discuss how to improve their technique. Then do it again. On your "go," see which group can complete the same task fastest the second time. Award a small prize, such as a bag of candies to share with everyone. After they sit down again, ask them what they did as a team to improve their time.

DISCUSSION

1. Some of your students have been through traumatic moments, and you want to be sensitive to those. You want to get students talking about how it felt to be very ill or injured. What was it like during that time? Did they ever feel like they'd never be well? Did they ever feel desperate? Some injuries and illnesses are with us our whole lives, and some may have family or friends who have died because of illness or injury.

2. Lepers were outcasts, not allowed to live among others (Numbers 5:1-4) and kept to very limited contact with the outside world. But Jesus actually touched the man with leprosy before healing him. That must have been an amazing moment for the leper, after being untouched for so long. Have students share their thoughts.

3. Ask students to share their scenes. Keep track of which moments from the story capture their attention. To help students reflect, help them think through the motivation and perspective of each principal character. What were their goals? What was the goal of the men who brought their friend? What did Jesus do?

4. Students can enter into this story by identifying with different characters. The people in the crowd were observers of the scene. The Pharisees and teachers were skeptical of who Jesus was, while one man lay before Jesus in need of healing. The men on the roof were friends who would do anything, including tearing up a roof, to get their friend to Jesus.

5. The Bible says Jesus noticed the faith of the friends and the sick man (verse 20). As you look over the list and your selections, imagine God was answering this question for you. What would God think you need? Would God have different answers?

CLOSE

Remind students about the opening game, where they worked together to lift four of their friends in the air—even getting a second chance to do it better. In the same way, we need to help each other as we try to be faithful to God. Sometimes we need forgiveness, other times we're in need of healing, and sometimes we just need good friends to support us through tough times. Close with prayer for your group, asking that they'll be the kind of people who help support one another and bring people to Jesus so that they can experience his healing forgiveness.

MORE

One of the questions people pose about Christianity is whether miracles occur or not. This is a valid question for your students to wrestle with as well—many students ask that same question in their minds. Don't run away from the opportunity to discuss it. If you open this up, you'll want to do some reading beforehand so you can be prepared for a variety of answers. There are some quick chapters on the idea in *The Case for Faith* and *The Case for Christ*, both by Lee Strobel. A great book on apologetics is *Building Belief* by Chad Meister (Baker). Open the discussion with a general question such as, "Why do people doubt that miracles are possible?"

1. For each pair, circle the word or phrase that best describes you whenever you have a bad cold or the flu. I like to…

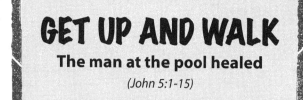

GET UP AND WALK
The man at the pool healed
(John 5:1-15)

Be by myself (or) complain to others.

Sleep a lot (or) watch TV.

Eat chicken noodle soup (or) take medicine.

Skip school (or) keep pushing on.

Feel like the world is going to end (or) be optimistic that I'll feel better tomorrow.

2. Why do you think that Jesus asks the man, "Do you want to get well?" in verse 6?

3. Read Mark 3:1-5. What was the main problem the religious leaders had with Jesus regarding these two miracles?

Is the idea of a Sabbath day important to your family?
What do you do to observe it?

4. Jesus found the man in the temple and reminded him to "stop sinning" or something worse might happen. What's a possible explanation of what this means?

___ The man was ungrateful and didn't change his ways.
___ Jesus would make him an invalid again if he didn't change.
___ Jesus was reminding him that the judgments of God were worse than being invalid.
___ The man was self-centered and didn't really understand who had healed him.

5. Finish this sentence: To demonstrate that I'm a Christian, each week I…

If Jesus walked up to me and said something, I think he'd say (select one):

"Do you want to get well?"
"I have come that you might have life to the full."
"Repent and believe, for the kingdom of God is in front of you."
"Come and follow me."
"Well done, good and faithful servant."

THIS WEEK

The desire to be healthy and happy is a powerful one, and a lot of time and money is spent working toward that goal. The reality is that we still get sick or injured. There's an inverse relationship between happiness and materialism—the more you acquire, the less satisfied you feel. Many people fall into the "if I only had this, then I'd be happy" lie. This TalkSheet focuses on a moment when Jesus encounters a man trying to get well by lying next to a healing pool.

OPENER

Divide your group into teams of six or so and tell them to create and perform a short infomercial for a product that will solve everyone's problems. It could be a new medicine (pill or shot), invention, or exercise that will make them healthier and happier. To jump-start the process, pass out to the teams slips of paper with four or five ideas on them. Give them five to seven minutes to come up with the infomercial and then have each group perform. What claims did each group make about their product? How are these claims similar to how people try to improve today? Are there other ways people try to be "healed" from problems?

DISCUSSION

1. This question should get students reflecting on how they respond to being sick. They can begin to identify with the man in this story. After students have shared their questions, read John 5:1-15. Ideally, have four people act it out as you read it. Bring a small blanket for the mat and have two people act as the Jewish leaders. You can either have the actors repeat the quotes or have them memorize them beforehand. Ask students what they observed in the scene as depicted.

2. Have students share their answers with the group. Have they ever met someone who enjoyed being sick and talking about it? Do they know anyone who loves to talk about what's hurting on their body? How do they feel when they're around them? Jesus asks an interesting question, and it helps the man to focus on the real issue—does he truly want to get well? Sometimes we know what we need to do to get well spiritually—we just don't want to do it.

3. The command to observe the Sabbath day each week is a strong one in the Old Testament (Exodus 20:8-11). In fact, to disobey the Sabbath was punishable by death (Numbers 15:32-36) and blessings were promised for observing it (Isaiah 58:13). Originally intended for humanity's refreshment, the Sabbath was weighted down by a list of dos and don'ts the religious leaders had added as they interpreted it. But Jesus confronted this list, as the Creator has the authority to do. After Pentecost, the church gathered on the first day of the week to worship, pray, and financially support the work of the church (Acts 20:7; 1 Corinthians 16:2; Revelation 1:10).

4. All but the second choice are possible answers. Take a quick poll on how many selected each statement to get an idea of your group's consensus. The first statement likely will be the most popular, so make sure to discuss the last two. Do they have any potential to be the best answer? Why or why not?

5. Have students share their answers to the first statement. What did they come up with? Does it look different from those who would say they aren't Christians? Do any of their families have Sunday traditions you occasionally do?

CLOSE

Have students look over their second answer to #5 and imagine what the scene might look like. Have them close their eyes and think more about what that encounter was like. What was the setting? The atmosphere? The emotions? Have students pray silently and encourage them to sit in silence, just listening. Close by reading John 10:10—"I have come that they may have life, and have it to the full."

MORE

• **One of the interesting themes in the early part of the book of John is the role water plays in describing God's work. At the wedding at Cana, Jesus changed common water used for washing into the best wine, and he also told the woman at the well in Samaria that he was the living water, which would satisfy her thirsty soul. Another man attempted to find healing in water, but only through Jesus could he experience what he needed. Explore this related idea of "thirsts" in our life—desires for more—and how we can experience contentment. (See Ecclesiastes 5:10; Psalm 16; or Philippians 4:11-12 for more on contentment.)**

• **For further discussion about the Sabbath, explore Colossians 2:16, which suggests there were various perspectives among Christians about what to do on the Sabbath. Christians were no longer observing Jewish laws for the seventh day of the week, but gathered on the first day of the week for prayer—yet still demonstrated a respect for the seventh day ("the Lord's day" of Rev. 1:10). Some churches meet on Saturday. The issue isn't when, but what. Should Christians observe a holy day each week? What should that look like? What should they do on that day?**

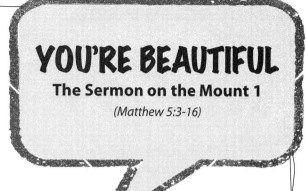

YOU'RE BEAUTIFUL

The Sermon on the Mount 1

(Matthew 5:3-16)

1. Grab one or two others and read through verses 3-10 of Matthew 5. As a group, select four of the verses and rewrite them so others can understand what they mean and how the short passage reflects the spirit of God.

Verse #   Your group's version

2. If someone eats a lot of salty foods, what happens?

Which do most people know more about—New York or Tucson, Arizona?

Why?

3. Read the first part of verse 14 again and then look up John 8:12. In what ways do these two verses make sense together? How can Christians be the light of the world if Jesus is the light?

4. Look over your rewritten versions of the four verses. Rank yourself next to each on a scale of 1 to 10 (10 being the highest) on how you've lived each verse over the past two weeks. How have you shown the character of Jesus to others?

THIS WEEK

One of the most beautiful things we can do for another person is to be kind and helpful. Any list of Christian qualities would include "kind" and "loving"—since Jesus was. This TalkSheet explores what those beautiful moments look like in a world that's anything but kind.

OPENER

Read Zechariah 4:6—"'Not by might nor by power, but by my Spirit,' says the LORD Almighty." Make two columns on the whiteboard, leaving room for a small third one in the middle. Title the left column "Our Own Might and Power" and the right one "By God's Spirit." Ask students to make a list of qualities in each column. What does it mean to act in our own might and power versus through God's Spirit? You may need to prompt your students a bit here.

Write the following in the small middle column and ask students what each item would look like in the other columns: being an example, attending church, helping others, and leading a group. Transition by asking, "Can the people watching these middle-column activities always tell a difference between the two columns?" Is it possible to have a great youth ministry through "might and power"? Today we'll look at a familiar passage to find out how each of these can be done in a way God desires versus our own "might and power."

DISCUSSION

1. Give students some time to complete this exercise. Build off the opening exercise and have students think about how they reflect Christ's love and purposes, as opposed to just trying to act good. Students may avoid verse 3, so make sure they consider the opposite of it: What does it mean to be "proud in spirit"? These verses are commonly called the Beatitudes, which means "the blesseds." They serve as a model for how those committed to Christ should behave.

   After students share some of their rewrites, have them share whether these are difficult or easy to do in their worlds.

2. Read verses 13-16. Salt adds flavor, but it also creates thirst. Historically, salt was also used to preserve food, not just to add flavor. Ask students, "If you have God's 'flavor' in your life, what kind of thirst should this create in others?" It should inspire people to look at our good deeds and give glory to (be thirsty for) God. Why is New York so famous? Because it's so big and important, it's like a city on a hill, impossible to ignore. Should we live our lives in such a way that others cannot ignore us, or should we fit in? What are the benefits and problems of both?

3. The goal for right behavior isn't to "be good" or to display for others how spiritual we are. The goal should be to reflect Jesus through how we live—that people will give credit to Christ for our kindness, helpfulness, and love. Is it difficult to act like Jesus when we want to fit in at school? Some take this too far, holding themselves apart from other people in a judgmental way. But the beatitudes are full of kindness to others and center on Jesus' ability to bring forgiveness and personal healing.

4. We don't live in a naturally kind world, and even within churches there can be cruelty. Most of the jokes on television are put-downs, and school interactions can be full of ridicule and sarcasm. What would happen if our particular youth group decided to work at reflecting Jesus' love toward others, and even toward one another? What would that look like? How could we support each other in such a process?

CLOSE

Jesus came to earth not just to die on the cross and rise again for the forgiveness of sins, but also to reveal more about who God is and how intense his love is for us. He showed us God's value to those whom the world and the religiously proud have rejected. The beatitudes open a section of Scripture called the Sermon on the Mount and provide a framework for how those committed to Christ should live. Close with prayer for your students, asking that they and you may reflect Jesus this week.

MORE

• **You may want to set up a random-acts-of-kindness weekend event. Your group can choose from a variety of helpful activities in their community—without expectation of a donation. Some groups pass out new water bottles to customers as they leave a local department store—others do work for needy people in the local church—and a simple one is a free car wash that's actually free.**

• **Challenge your students to perform 10 helpful actions this next week at home, school, or work. Pass out sheets with nice graphics and 10 spots to write down what they did to be helpful, kind, or a blessing to someone else. Tell students to think about the *most helpful* actions they could take, not necessarily the *easiest*. Remind students to help intelligently—in a way that the helpee appreciates. The following week, have people report back on how they chose to bless others.**

1. What does it mean to be a Christian?

What does a Christian do that makes him or her a Christian?

2. People give money for a variety of reasons. Why have you given money? Check all that apply.

___ For someone on their birthday

___ As a tithe/offering to church

___ To support missions   ___ In secret—to help someone else

___ To a relative in need   ___ So that God will bless with more

___ To obey God   ___ To support a good cause

3. Complete the following, "In the last week, I prayed ___ times other than at a meal."

The three most common things I prayed for are:

1.

2.

3.

Look over Jesus' prayer in verses 9-13. What did Jesus pray about?

4. Define what it means to fast.

Have you ever purposely gone without something important for a period of time? List it below and explain what happened:

5. If you were to answer the question, "What does it mean to be a Christian?" again, what would you want to add or change now?

Do some people misunderstand what it means to be a Christian? Explain:

THIS WEEK

It is easy to view being a Christian as something we *do* versus a relationship we enter into through faith and God's grace. Our actions and our faith commitment are connected, and Jesus was concerned about the reasons why we do what we do. Many religious people in his day acted spiritual, but lacked right motives and faith in God. This TalkSheet exposes students to well-known spiritual practices and what Jesus says about them.

OPENER

Divide your group into four teams, giving a section of this chapter to each. Give each team a title and a passage: Giving—Matthew 6:1-4; Prayer—Matthew 6:5-8; Fasting—Matthew 6:16-18; Money—Matthew 6:19-24. They're to come up with a live two-minute skit (or YouTube video, if that helps) that illustrates the passage with a modern example. (If you want, prep a couple of ideas ahead of time in case any teams get stuck.) Each team should choose a narrator to read the passage and take five to seven minutes to work on ideas. Then have them perform their skit or show their video. After all the performances are over, ask students to respond to them.

DISCUSSION

1. Have students share their responses. You'll get a variety of responses to the first question because students will interpret it differently. That's okay—you'll learn about how they each think as they share. For the second question, ask students, "If someone says they're a swimmer, but they haven't been swimming in six months, are they really a swimmer? So what is it that we do that makes us Christian? Is there anything we have to do?" Let students share their perspectives on this without correcting them. The answer to this question will vary from leader to leader and church to church.

2. Do people give money for all these reasons? Which ones are the best reasons? Read Matthew 6:2-3. What is Jesus saying about how we should give?

What was Jesus trying to confront? What reward were the boasting givers seeking? What reward should we seek when we give?

3. Ask students to silently look over their answers. If they were to write a prescription to help their prayer life, what would it be? Tell students to quietly write their prescription along the right side of their paper and to include two action steps.

4. Fasting is skipping physical food in order to focus on spiritual food. It's more than just skipping a meal, it's also adding in a time of special spiritual discipline such as Bible reading or prayer to provide spiritual nourishment. Can we fast from something other than food? What about a media fast? Or a single-food fast (soda, chocolate, pizza, beets) for a longer period of time?

5. What happens when we lose sight of what Jesus sees as spiritual? How did the Pharisees mess up what God intended? What causes us to get self-centered in our reasons for going to church, praying, reading the Bible, or "doing" Christian practices?

CLOSE

Encourage students to recommit themselves to fostering their spiritual lives in the midst of schedules and lives that work against that. Challenge students to be tough on themselves as they think about the things they do just so others see them as being "good Christians." Close by leading your group in the Lord's Prayer.

MORE

The concept of what defines a person as a Christian is an important one for teens and adults to think through—it's more than a one-time decision. It's an ongoing reliance on and faith in Jesus Christ. It's also important to combat doubt, to focus on important practices, and to understand God's grace. You may want to have students examine what the Apostle Paul said in 2 Corinthians 11:16-30; Galatians 6:14-15; and 1 Timothy 1:15-16. Have students list how Paul defined what it meant for him to be a Christian. How does that list compare to how most Christians today define themselves?

1. The first part of verse 25 means, "Don't be anxious about your life." How would you describe what this means to a friend?

TRUST
The Sermon on the Mount 3
(Matthew 6:25-34)

2. When you were four to seven years old, what fears or worries did you have? Think of three or four worries and write them below:

What do you worry or get scared about most now?

3. Read John 14:27. What would peace look like in your life? In your relationship with God? In your relationship with others? In your thinking about yourself? Write down what comes to your mind:

Read John 14:1. How might trust in God keep your heart from being troubled?

4. Team up with two or three others and read Matthew 7:24-27. What two options does Jesus give his listeners?

Describe what Jesus says is the wise option:

5. What is the most difficult aspect of putting your trust in God for all areas of your life?

In which area is the most difficult for you to trust God?

THIS WEEK

At the end of the Sermon on the Mount is a gentle invitation from Jesus for his listeners to trust in God. It can be difficult to do in an age of self-sufficiency, and for students who are still discovering who God is—particularly in light of some students' relationships with earthly fathers who may be untrustworthy.

OPENER

Tell students you're going to make the floor into a worry scale. Those who worry a lot can move to the right of the room. Those who never worry should move toward the left side. Those who say they're in the middle—which shouldn't be many—can stand in the middle of the room. The rest need to stand wherever they are on the worry scale somewhere between the right and left walls. Tell students to be prepared to explain where they are on the scale. They may need to talk about specific instances to make sure they're exactly where they need to be on the scale. Play some instrumental upbeat music while they work on this. After five minutes, stop the music and have a fast-paced discussion—you want to hear why students put themselves where they are on the worry scale and whether they're truly in the right spot. When finished, have students return to their original spots.

DISCUSSION

1. Get students talking about anxiety. It's a safe concept to discuss, but you'll probably find it's a big issue for students, though they may not know it! Anxiety is common today, and teenagers seem to suffer most. What does it mean to not be anxious in our own lives? Isn't it impossible to not be anxious? Is anxiousness okay, or is it a sign of a serious problem?

2. Ask students what they do when they're anxious. Are any of them pacers? Do they bite their fingernails? Do they lose sleep when they're uptight? Do some get angry or go and hide from the problem? Do any of them pursue habits (video games, sleep) to try to numb the anxiety?

3. In this passage, Jesus comforts his disciples after they found out about the coming betrayal and Jesus' leaving them. This is a reflective question, so you may need to do some prompting. Read Romans 5:1 to help students think about their relationship with God. You may want to have these verses on an overhead for students to consider. Hebrews 12:14 relates to living at peace with others. Ask students if they thought about being at peace with themselves. Is that difficult or easy?

4. Jesus gives two options. Are there others? Is it possible to build on a solid foundation partially or occasionally? Have students describe what they think of when they think of a wise person. What does wisdom look like? Why is it wise to trust God for the future?

5. Tell students that all have areas in their lives where it's difficult to surrender and let God be God. What is it that causes this worry? How does an understanding that God is in charge help (or not help) with moments of worry?

CLOSE

Have students close their eyes and reflect on their level of fear, worry, and mistrust that things will be okay. Remind them of some areas as they reflect—family, work, school, sports, friends, dating life, future. After a minute, tell students to imagine that Jesus sits down with them and talks about these matters. What would he say? What would that scene be like? What would the setting be, the tone of voice, the nonverbal expressions?

MORE

• **Before starting this exercise, set a series of signs or images around the room representing some chief concerns in life, such as a good job, healthy family, good diet, trendy clothes, following God's will, money, fun, vacations, and so on. In front of each sign, put a bowl or box. Feel free to get creative, but don't have more than 10 stations.**

• **Then divide your group into equal teams of no more than eight per team. Give each team an equal amount of play money ($100 works well). Tell students to spend their play money on what's important to their group. Each team can establish the worth of the different areas before they spend their total. They may determine that a good job is worth $30 of their total, so they put $30 of the play money in that box. When all the teams are done, have someone go around and total what was spent at each sign.**

• **Worry can often be a symptom of a larger issue in life, like a poor parent/child relationship or an inability to trust others or God. This passage reassures the students that the Father feeds them (verse 26), the Father clothes them (verse 30), and the Father knows them (verse 32). You can use other passages such as Matthew 6:8; Philippians 4:6; and 1 Peter 5:7 to discuss anxiety and worry with your students.**

1. Imagine that Jesus has chosen to come and speak to your school at an assembly, and the principal of your school has given you the task of introducing him. What would you say? Write down two or three phrases you'd want to be sure to include:

AN UNUSUAL VOICE

John the Baptist

(Mark 1:1-8; John 1:29-34)

2. John the Baptist was given the responsibility to introduce Jesus to the world. Get in a group with three or four other people and pretend you're in need of a prophet for a marketing program. Create a job description of what John did. Look up Isaiah 40:3; Malachi 3:1; Mark 1:1-8; and John 1:29-34 and base your two or three sentences on what these verses say about John's job. Be creative!

3. In Luke 7:18-19, John has some moments of doubt in prison about whether Jesus is really the Messiah. It's not uncommon to see characters in the Bible struggle with doubt. What's the difference between doubt and unbelief?

4. Rate yourself on how often you have doubts about Jesus and who the Bible says he is:

◀ •• ▶

I don't doubt
that much

Probably
average

I have lots
of doubts

Briefly explain why you ranked yourself at that point:

5. Jesus praised John the Baptist as being among the greatest prophets of all time. Which of the following best describes why you think Jesus defended John to his followers even when John had questions:

❑ They were wondering why a prophet of God was in prison.
❑ In spite of John's uncertainty, he never wavered in his belief.
❑ John was near the end of life and just wanted to know for sure about Jesus.
❑ Jesus is a forgiver and is able to forgive those who doubt.
❑ John's ministry was a great sign that Jesus was the Messiah.
❑ John was considered the last and greatest of the prophets.

THIS WEEK

The life and story of John the Baptist is often over-looked, yet his ministry was an important sign that Jesus was the Messiah and that he would establish the kingdom of God. This TalkSheet introduces students to the story of John the Baptist and helps them reflect on their own moments of doubt.

OPENER

Have everyone in your group find a partner, preferably someone they don't know that well. Have each pair determine who's younger and announce that you're giving the younger students one minute to learn as much as they can about the other person. After one minute, announce that the older students in each pair now have one minute to find out as much as they can about the younger person. At the end of that minute, have each pair connect with another pair so there are now four people in each group. Now give each person 30 seconds to introduce his or her partner to the other two. Make sure you encourage the students to be both creative and thorough in their introductions. After two or three minutes of introductions are up, you may want to informally ask from up front who thought someone in their group had a particularly good introduction. If the person is willing, have her or him stand and introduce the partner to the entire group.

Opening question for the large group: No doubt many of you have been in places where someone is introduced. Why do people introduce others? What's the purpose of an introduction?

DISCUSSION

1. After students have written for a few minutes, tell them that how one person thinks about Jesus can be very different from how others think—even the person next to us! This doesn't mean one person is wrong and one is right—it just shows that our experiences and personalities allow us to value different areas of who Jesus is. Have students volunteer to share their phrases. Write down the main ideas of each phrase on the whiteboard. As students share what others have said, put a mark after that idea to keep a tally.
2. Have some fun with this part. John the Baptist was a man totally committed to God and to his ministry. He was radical in how he looked, what he ate, and what he said. Have a member from each group share their job descriptions. At the conclusion of this part,

remind students about John's deep commitment to preparing the way for the Messiah.
3. Though John was deeply committed to God, the Bible shows us he also struggled with doubt. Like Moses, Elijah, Jeremiah, and even Paul, people committed to God can struggle with moments of despair—but that doesn't mean they've given up their trust. Allow some students to share their definitions. You may want to summarize by pointing out that doubt usually comes when we aren't sure what God's doing. Unbelief comes when we snub God and choose not to believe in his Word. How did being stuck in a prison affect John emotionally and physically? How does physical and emotional pain change our own perspective?
4. Have students put a mark where they think God would rank them. Then have them reflect on why they put that mark where they did. Why did they put that second mark where they did? What do their answers say about their perspective of God? How do these answers compare to the ones they gave in question 1? Are there differences? Why?
5. Ask for a quick show of hands for each of these. All five are possible reasons, but it'll be interesting to see which answer got the most responses among your students.

CLOSE

At the beginning of this lesson, we focused on introducing Jesus to others. At the end we recognized there may be occasional doubts we have with being a Christian. Have students review their answers for question #1 and remind your students that those are the enduring qualities that come to mind when they think of who Jesus is in their lives. Remind students they need to live so their actions introduce people to Jesus.

MORE

• **For a bit of fun at the beginning, edit a videotape of introductions from any talk show or awards show—10 to 12 really quick introductions that are particularly funny, serious, or really cheesy. It'll make a fun opening and get your lesson off a good start. It'll take time, but a student or adult with skills could do it quickly.**
• **If you want more depth, Jesus' reply to John's uncertainty was carefully worded. It was a direct reference to Isaiah 53:5-6 and Isaiah 61:6—prophecies that concerned the signs and purposes of the Messiah's ministry. What signs and purposes should a Christian's life show so that others know who Jesus is? What should we do when we have doubts?**

1. There are two people in this story besides Jesus. Based on today's story and what you know from other stories in the Bible, describe each of them.

Simon, the Pharisee

The repentant woman

2. Read Luke 7:16 and then verse 39. Why do you think the Pharisee invited Jesus to his house?

What was Jesus' response and how did this show that he was a prophet?

3. Write down two times where you wronged someone (a parent, friend, coach, or teacher) and found yourself in big trouble. For each one, describe how you received forgiveness.

TROUBLE TIME   HOW WERE YOU FORGIVEN?

4. Put an X next to the one answer you think best describes what sin is.

_____ Missing the mark (Hosea 13:2; Romans 6:12; James 1:15)

_____ Rebelling against God (Exodus 23:33; 1 Kings 8:50; Matthew 7:23)

_____ Twisting what God intended (Psalm 51:4; Daniel 9:5; Romans 8:7)

Read Colossians 2:13-14. What did Jesus do that allows him to forgive sins, canceling our debt?

5. What did Jesus say was the reason the woman's sins were forgiven?

Where would you put yourself on this scale below in how you've responded to Jesus and his offer to forgive you of your sins?

◀ • ▶

Like the Pharisee,
indifferent, skeptical,
uninformed, proud

Like the woman,
emotional, aware,
humble, broken

THIS WEEK

This lesson is a vivid illustration of God's compassion, love, and forgiveness for those who put their faith in Jesus Christ. This TalkSheet helps students develop their understanding of sin, a prominent biblical theme, and of how God extends forgiveness to those who respond to his love through faith and repentance.

OPENER

What sin is the "worst"? Have students discuss this in order to "rank" sins. Ask students to list 15 to 20 sins and write them on the board. Have students divide them into three groups by telling you which are considered by society as the worst, which are in between, and which are considered not a big deal. Some students may point out that all sins are equal since all sin is disobedience to God. Help students think by asking whether or not some actions involve more than one sin—such as murder or sexual sin. Challenge students to include the foundational sins of pride, envy, and jealousy. Where would they rank? Do they cause any of the other sins? Can God forgive all of these? Tell students you're going to read a story of forgiveness in which Jesus forgives someone's debt in the presence of a proud religious person. Read the story in Luke 7:36-50.

DISCUSSION

1. Tell students to include in their descriptions aspects like motivation, social standing, and other less obvious characteristics. When finished, have students share what they wrote. Make two columns on the whiteboard. You'll probably see a serious of sharp opposites between the two columns. When finished, ask students which of the two was a sinner? The answer is both, of course, because Simon was proud and unaware of his own sin (Luke 18:9-14, for example) and we're all sinners (Romans 3:23).

2. Simon the Pharisee was seen as an important person, and an invitation for Jesus to eat in his home was a significant event in that neighborhood. Uninvited people could come, too, but had to stand in the background to watch and listen. This woman wouldn't have been allowed in the Pharisee's house except for the fact that Jesus was there. Is there a modern-day equivalent for this setting? Since the woman lived in that town, yet still broke social customs, what does it say about her faith?

3. Encourage students to be honest—no one's going to ask them to share what they wrote. Once students have two, ask them what it felt like to be forgiven for each one. Did they experience a sense of peace? Did anyone feel they *hadn't* been forgiven for that? It's difficult for us to truly forgive. Those who were forgiven—how did it feel after that? Was there a sense of peace, a sense that everything was okay? How did you get that?

4. Whom did the Pharisee recognize as owing the greater debt? Jesus noted that the Pharisee was self-important and, when contrasted with the woman's humble response, didn't extend to him the usual customs of hospitality to guests. The debt for sin is death (Romans 6:23), but the gift of God is eternal life with him when we put our faith in him (Romans 10:9, 10) and follow him.

5. Is it faith or love that saves people from their sins (Ephesians 2:8-9)? How have you responded to God's love by putting your faith in him—and how is that expressed?

CLOSE

This story provides a great opportunity for us to examine our own lives and respond to Jesus and his Spirit. Have students look over their answers to the last question and tell them you're going to give them an opportunity to respond to God today. You can either lead them in a prayer of confession or pass out 3 x 5 cards and have them write a prayer to God. Offer students who want to commit their lives to Christ the opportunity to meet in another room. Whatever you do, close by allowing an opportunity for students to pray for forgiveness, to experience Christ's love for the first time, or to consider their own response to God's leading in their lives.

MORE

• **The woman's actions were dramatic as she expressed her love for Jesus. Is it difficult for you to demonstrate your love for God? Is it easier in private or in public? In what ways do people today demonstrate it? How did the woman know her sins were forgiven? How do we know our sins are forgiven (Acts 13:38-39; 1 John 1:9; and Hebrews 8:12)?**
• **Galatians 5:6 says, "The only thing that counts is faith expressing itself through love." Is it faith or love that saves people from their sins (Ephesians 2:8-9)? What are some ways that "faith expressing itself through love" looks in each person's life? In your youth group?**

BE CAREFUL WHAT YOU SAY
Jesus warns the Pharisees
(Matthew 12:33-37)

1. For each of the following, rate yourself on a scale of 1 to 10, with 10 being "a lot like me" and 1 being "not like me at all."

_____ I keep my promises.

_____ I keep my New Year's resolutions.

_____ I like to sound cool and use the latest catch-phrases that others use.

_____ I talk differently at school than I do at church.

_____ The words I use changes depending on which groups of friends I am around.

_____ I like to sound like I know what I'm talking about.

_____ I speak up when I need to.

_____ I can easily say "I'm sorry" and admit that I'm wrong.

2. Read Matthew 12:22-24. What did the Pharisees say about Jesus?

What did Jesus say in verses 25-28?

3. Rewrite the following verses in your own words.

Psalm 19:14

2 Timothy 2:14

4. Is it easy or difficult for you to honestly share your deepest feelings with your friends? Why?

With parents?

With your church leaders?

With God?

5. Do you think people are careful or careless in what they say to God?

What commitments have you made to God?

THIS WEEK

The subjects we choose to talk about and the words we use say a lot about what's important to us. It doesn't take much time watching television to realize that what we laugh at and choose to quote isn't always the most God-honoring stuff. That can carry over into our conversations and, before we know it, we're talking in ways that may not reflect what God desires. This TalkSheet enables students to discuss their speech in light of Jesus' teaching and to realize that what they say can be a blessing or a curse to others.

OPENER

Ask students which television show or movie they quote the most. Are certain quotes from movies or television shows part of their everyday conversation?

What do your students think of when they think of the phrase "empty words"? What are idle or empty words you hear people use? Are slang words considered empty? What are some of the "in" words or phrases students use? List them on the board. Feel free to add words that were popular in previous decades and get some reactions. What about "Christian cussing"— saying words that sound close to swear words? Are they careless or idle words (Ephesians 5:4)?

Now take your students in a new direction. What about sarcastic comments? Promises we don't keep? Promises to God that we don't follow? What about telling someone "I love you" when you mean something else? How can a vow that's made but not honored be the same as an idle word? How is it different? Discuss with students the role television and movies play in our conversations and what effect they have on what we say.

DISCUSSION

1. Let students share a bit about what they noticed from their rankings. Was there any one item that was difficult to decide? Is it difficult for them to be careful of what they say? Make sure they can share honestly without fear of being ridiculed or thought of as different.

2. The Pharisees were getting more concerned about Jesus and his teaching, and they tried to explain where Jesus got his power. In the same way, what are some things people say about God that aren't true? If we followed the advice in these two verses, what would change? Have you ever changed how you talked or what words you choose? Do you consciously choose not to say some words or phrases?

3. What did your students come up with on these rewrites? What are the principles in each of these verses? What would happen if they put these principles into practice? Is it even a big deal to be careful of what we say?

4. Get students talking about what role words play in their lives. Have they sent a text message or email that was misunderstood? Why did that misunderstanding happen? Many times it's because the receiver wasn't able to read any nonverbal communication. What makes it difficult to talk about how we feel with others? Why is it easier to communicate in writing (letters, text, IM, email) than face-to-face? What makes talking more "real"?

5. Ask students whether they think people are careful or careless in what they say to God. Ask for examples of each. We don't often think about what we say in our relationship with God. We can make promises to God— Numbers 30 calls them vows—yet sometimes we fail to follow through on those commitments. It's important for us to review what promises we've made to God. It's also important to remind students what promises God has made to us. You may want to ask students what they feel that God has communicated to them in life. Do they feel God is leading them in some direction? How have they responded to that leading?

CLOSE

The principle from today is that words have power. While we can be careless with words, they can also have significant positive impact. The Scriptures give many examples of a spoken blessing having great significance. The New Testament contains examples of spoken benedictions—a blessing or encouragement to an audience as they're dismissed. You may want to close by reading one of these (Romans 5:5-6, 13, 33 or Hebrews 13:20-21) and then praying for your students that their words this week would reflect the meditation of their hearts.

MORE

• Help your students discover how words change by having a slang competition. Beforehand, find 10 "in" words you used in your teens as well as words commonly used before your time, and list them on a sheet of paper with room for students to write in their meaning after each one. For help, check out www.onlineslangdictionary.com and www.alphadictionary.com/slang for usable words. Make sure you're discerning and appropriate in all the words you use. Start by asking students for some of the "in" phrases they hear at school (appropriate ones). List these words and their meanings on the whiteboard. Now tell students you're going to give them a quiz of cool words commonly used in the past.

• For some further Bible study on words and what we say, check out Deuteronomy 23:21, 23; Numbers 30:1-4 on vows; Isaiah 57:3-4; Psalm 89:34; and Proverbs 10:11; 15:4; and 17:27-28. What do these verses say about our speech?

1. For each pair below, put a check next to the one that gets the most attention on how it looks for you and your family:

___ Front yard / Back yard ___

___ Outside of car / Inside of car ___

___ Family room / Bedroom ___

___ Clothes / Physical health ___

___ Actions at school / Actions at home ____

___ My reputation / My character ____

___ How we act at church / Our personal spiritual life ___

LOOKING GOOD ON THE OUTSIDE
The six woes
(Luke 11:39-52)

2. Read Luke 11:42-44. What did the Pharisees do?

What did they neglect?

3. Read the following verses and write down what the scribes did that Jesus confronted:

Verse 46—

Verse 47—

Verse 52—

4. Based on your reading today, which of the following people would you say is a hypocrite?

Juan attends church each week and would say he is a committed Christian. He occasionally reads his Bible, but has difficulty controlling his mouth, especially when he's around his friends. He tries to work on it, but it has been a problem for him.

Lori goes to church and likes to see all her friends there. She goes to all the youth group events, but doesn't really connect with what's going on. She tells all her friends she's a Christian, but when she's away from her church friends, she acts very differently.

Rudy sings in a choir for Christian athletes. It tours the local community, singing in various churches where the people give testimonies about their faith in God. After the concert, Rudy heads out to smoke pot with his friends who aren't in the choir. He tries to hide it from his friends in the choir, but some of them know about it.

5. What might Jesus say "woe to you" about in your life? Is there an area of secrecy you're hiding from others and trying to hide from God?

THIS WEEK

A common excuse for people is that they don't go to church or believe in God because the Christians they know are just a bunch of hypocrites—people who pretend to be Christian, but usually act very differently. This TalkSheet tackles that topic, showing what it meant in Jesus' day and connecting it to where students are today.

OPENER

What's the most religious-seeming thing we can do in our group? Have students rank these on a scale of 1 to 10 (10 being most religious) as you write them on the board:

attend church each week
have daily devotions
go on a short-term mission trip
act good
dress up when you go to church
say prayers before meals
carry your Bible to church
sing the worship music loudly

When finished, ask students, "Are any of these important to do?" Let students answer. Why are they important? After a few answers, ask students, "Which ones can be done for the wrong reasons?" Let students select which ones. In reality, all of them can be done for the wrong reasons; have students explain how and why. Ask students, too, if they've ever been evaluated by the way they do any of these activities. This is an important conversation, because students may feel a pressure to perform to fit into their youth ministry group. Transition by pointing out that Jesus confronted the Pharisees and others about the pride and performance of their spiritual lives.

DISCUSSION

1. What do students notice about their choices? Is there a leaning toward the outward, external areas, as opposed to private areas that fewer people regularly see? Why does it seem as if people are more concerned with externals than with areas that aren't seen by others? Read Luke 11:38-39 to set the scene for students.

2. The Pharisees were so strict in their religiosity that they even tithed on herbs and spices while ignoring those in need (Micah 6:7-8). They loved to impress others with their presence. Jesus was critical of them when he said the Pharisees were perpetually un-

clean (Numbers 19:16), as if they'd been around dead bodies—a comment that particularly upset them. Because so many people were buried in unmarked graves, they were often whitewashed so people could avoid coming in contact with them.

3. Jesus confronted the scribes on their ability to load people with rules, to celebrate past prophets without learning from their teaching, and to make it difficult for others to learn. Abel (Genesis 4:10) was the first one killed in the Old Testament—and Zechariah (2 Chronicles 24:22) was the last, according to how the Hebrew Bible is arranged. How do your students learn the Bible today? How do they learn what it means to be a Christian? Ask students what they think about each of these three. They'll hopefully generate some good conversation for your students. How did your students determine what is or isn't hypocrisy? Note that Rudy never claims to be a Christian—it's just assumed, since he's in the choir. Ask your students whether their church is full of hypocrites or not, based on their definition of what it means to be a hypocrite.

4. Challenge students to get with a trusted Christian adult (you?) in the next two weeks to talk about the challenge of living clean on both the outside and inside. Let them know you're available, as are other youth group leaders, and that it's a safe conversation—you won't pile on heavy loads.

CLOSE

Read Psalm 51:10-12 and close with prayer. Have students write down the area they thought of for question #5 on a small slip of paper and then put it in a large cup that's dirty on the inside—a symbol of recognition that the area isn't clean and that they're offering it to God, leaving it behind as they go home.

MORE

A week or more before this lesson, leave an inch (2.5 cm) of coffee in the bottom of a clean cup and let it sit. It'll grow mold and become like tar. Don't let students see inside, but hold it up and ask if anyone would like to take a drink. Few will decide to drink from the cup without first looking inside. It's not the outside of a cup that matters, but the inside. Do Christians put too much emphasis on the outside? Doesn't the outside (our actions and words) reveal what's going on inside? What are the inside issues people need to work on?

1. How helpful are you? Rate yourself below.

◀ • ▶

I love to help
and it's easy to do so.

It's hard for me
to help others.

2. If something happened to you in a public place such as a mall or restaurant, what type of person would be the least likely to help you? Describe the person:

What do you imagine would make this person unlikely to help you?

3. Read Luke 10:25-37. The priest and the Levite avoided the man. Why would they do that? See Leviticus 21:1-3 for help.

4. The expert said that the Samaritan showed mercy (verse 37). Read each of the following and write what it says about mercy.

      Ephesians 2:4—

      Hebrews 4:16—

      James 3:17—

5. Imagine you stepped in to help in each of the following situations. Which act of helpfulness would show the greatest amount of mercy?

    ___ A woman spills a bag of groceries in the parking lot and they roll all over.

    ___ A church bulletin announcement asks for volunteers to help landscape all day on a Saturday.

    ___ A new kid at your school regularly sits by himself or herself in the cafeteria.

    ___ On a short-term mission trip, a guy is begging outside your hotel.

    ___ Outside your local Wal-Mart, a guy holds a "Will work for food" sign.

    ___ Your mom or dad asks you to do the dishes and clean up the kitchen.

    ___ The neighbor's kids are always coming over to see what you're doing.

THIS WEEK

One of the basic ways we can be kind to others is by being helpful. We're to love God, but also to love one another, a command that requires kindness to others and an awareness of their needs. Yet basic helpfulness is often not a part of the regular habits of Christians. This TalkSheet takes a familiar story that Jesus told and challenges students—and teachers!—about their helpfulness.

OPENER

Tell students that you're going to check on how helpful they are through a Good Samaritan Quiz. For each scenario, they'll be given three options and they're to move to the part of the room that represents the option they would choose. Have students stand and read each option and then have students move to the designated spot. Feel free to make observations in an appropriate, nonsarcastic way about the group's choices.

• Your mom reminds you to clean your room. Do you do it right away, put it off till later in the day, or argue that it's clean enough?

• Someone's books and papers fall all over the hallway at school. Do you laugh, immediately help pick the books and papers up, or feel good because you knocked them out of the person's hands?

• When there's an obvious job to be done around the house, are you reluctant to help, wait to be asked, or act to do it before your parents have to do it?

• If you saw a guy in the Wal-Mart parking lot asking for gas money, would you give it to him, ignore him, or get mad because he's bugging you?

• When your church or school has a service day in your town, do you make sure you can show up to help, see if it fits into your schedule, or assume that others will cover it?

Remind students that it's easy to read about being helpful or to serve at a youth group event, but it's another thing to actually serve in our everyday lives.

DISCUSSION

1. The opener will have set this up well. Have students share how they determined where to put themselves on this scale. What scenes came to their minds?
2. Ask students for the kind of person they described and why. What factors did they use to determine who wouldn't help them? What barriers did they identify as important in determining whether someone would help them? Tell students that Jesus used such a person to challenge his listeners to love one another.

Read Luke 10:25-37. The Samaritan was someone the expert wouldn't want to help.

3. Have students share their answers. The two men in the story avoided the injured man because he would've made them ceremonially unclean even though they had the time and opportunity to help. What are some of the excuses people use today? So, an outcast—a Samaritan—stopped and helped the man. Do your students believe Christians are any more helpful than non-Christians? Can your students give examples?
4. The Bible is full of reminders and stories that demonstrate God has been merciful to us—so we should be merciful to others. How is not helping someone similar to judging them? Have students share some of the barriers that keep them from showing mercy to others. To keep this going, have them suggest ways they show mercy to those in their home. List their answers on the whiteboard.
5. There really isn't a right answer for this one. In fact, you may want to ask whether or not there are greater amounts of mercy. Did any of these situations seem to not be about mercy? Allow students to share their opinions and reasons.

CLOSE

The story of the Good Samaritan is so well-known that most people know what it means to be a Good Samaritan. Why is it so difficult to do this in our everyday lives? What would the results be if we all put into practice the ability to help others, even those who are outcasts? Have students share some ideas and write them on the board. Drill down more and ask students what would have to change in their lives for this to happen. Close with prayer.

MORE

• **For more on helpfulness, have students read any of the following: Acts 20:36; 1 Thessalonians 5:14; 1 Timothy 6:2; Titus 3:5. The command to love the "Lord your God" comes from Deuteronomy 6:5, whereas the command to love one another comes from Leviticus 19:18.**

• **One of the final episodes of the television show "Seinfeld" (Episode 179, Season 9) centered on the four main characters watching a guy being robbed—and not helping in any way. They were arrested because they broke a Good Samaritan law. Make sure to screen it first, but you can show it to prompt a discussion on whether this really happens today. What would they have done in a real-life situation?**

• **Preview a great YouTube video that may challenge your students before the opener: www.youtube.com/watch?v=lcK2iaT3TkU.**

1. Rank the following 10 types of people on their level of honesty. Who is the most honest (give them a 10) and who is the most dishonest (a 1)? Rank the others from 2 to 9.

_____ Friends at school   _____ Police officer

_____ TV newscaster   _____ Parents

_____ Politician   _____ Clergyperson

_____ Actor   _____ Me

_____ Reality show   _____ Salesperson at store
          participant

SECRETS AND THE SON
(Luke 12:2-10)

2. Read Luke 12:2, 3. What does Jesus say will happen to things done in secret?

What do you think his motivation is for teaching this?

Read 1 Corinthians 4:5. What does this say to the pretender—someone who is quite different when he's away from others?

Circle Y or N—Is there something you've whispered in secret that you'd be nervous to have exposed?

3. Get with two or three others around you, read Luke 12:8-10, and rewrite the verses in your own words so that this is set in current culture.

4. Rank yourself below. How open are you able to be with the following people? Put a "P" on the line below for parents, "C" for people at church, "F" for friends, and "Y" for yourself.

◀ • ▶

I am very open   I keep things hidden

5. What is God trying to do in your life right now? Are there areas of secrecy you need to give up trying to hide? Spend a few moments writing down what comes to mind as you reflect on these questions.

THIS WEEK

Jesus challenged his listeners to not merely play a part and act like his followers, but he also reminded them that God sees everything and that after they die, there will be an examination of their lives. This TalkSheet will help students discuss God's awareness of how they choose to live each day, both as he cares for them and as he's aware of their secrets.

OPENER

Kick off this discussion by asking your high schoolers to explain how, in a relationship, trusting the other person allows them to be more honest. How is trust earned? How is it given? If your students were in a relationship and the other person lied or revealed a secret, what would they do? Get various responses from your students and write them on the board. Keep this moving and upbeat. Read Luke 12:2-10 to your students. Ask, "Do Christians generally try to hide their relationship with God, or be open about it?" In what ways should Christians be truthful with their friends about God? Write this list on the board, too. Kick off this discussion by summarizing this opening section and reminding your students that it's because of God's love, as expressed in his power, knowledge, and in his Son, Jesus Christ, that we can trust him and acknowledge him in all areas of our lives—our private actions, our public witness, and our words.

DISCUSSION

1. This question should spark a lot of conversation. Which person did they find was the most dishonest? The most honest? Was there a consensus in your group about these? What criteria did the students use to determine honesty? Was it easy or difficult to figure out who was honest?

2. Jesus wanted his listeners to examine their lives using the example of the Pharisees' hypocrisy—acting religious on the outside, but rejecting God and his love. Do your students think most people know that God sees their every moment or not? Do they know God is aware that all will be made known after life is over? Why do they think most people have secret areas of their lives they think are hidden from others?

3. Get some of your groups to share what they wrote. What does it mean to publicly acknowledge Jesus? When is this easy? Difficult? What does it mean to disown Christ? How did your students interpret verse 10? Have the following verses written on an overhead or on the board—2 Corinthians 1:22; 2 Corinthians 3:18; and Galatians 5:16. What is the role of the Holy Spirit in the lives of Christians? How does rejecting his work lead to not being forgiven?

4. With whom did students feel most comfortable being open? As they put the "Y" on the scale for themselves individually, what thoughts were they thinking? Were they thinking of specific moments in the past? What criteria were used to determine where each person stood with each group? Spend some time teasing these out a bit.

5. You may need to help students think about these three questions, giving them some time to complete this a second time. Have them focus on areas where they've known they may need to be more obedient to what God wants.

CLOSE

Jesus noted that the hypocrisy of the Pharisees was like yeast, a small ingredient used to make bread rise. It represented two negatives: It was considered bad since it ruined unleavened bread, and its puffed-up result reminded people of ego and pride. Once we begin to get comfortable with lies and deception in our lives, they can grow—unless they're surrendered and given to God. If you were creating a recipe for your life, what ingredients would you need to mix in to have God's flavor? What ingredients would ruin the flavor? Close by passing out homemade chocolate chip cookies or good bread. Once everyone has a piece, read Psalm 34:8, 11-14 as they eat.

MORE

• As a fun door game, have students guess how many hair follicles are on the average person's head. They can put their answers in a jar. Give a bottle of shampoo to the winner. (The answer is 100,000.) For an added video effect, play a video of a sparrow the whole time on a TV screen somewhere in the room. There are a few on YouTube. How much do your students pay attention to birds? Discuss with students one of the most profound images of how much God loves us, found in verses 6 and 7: Not one sparrow falls without God's knowledge. More than a sparrow, we're on God's radar so intimately that he knows things beyond our knowledge, such as how many hairs are on our head.

• Verse 10 is often called the unpardonable sin and can generate questions about what sin is unforgivable. Some writers say Jesus was speaking to those in that country who were resisting God's Spirit. Though God forgives those who earnestly seek forgiveness, people still have the free choice to reject and resist the work of the Holy Spirit so that they are not ultimately forgiven (John 3:36). Have students read John 16:7-15 about what the Holy Spirit does and have them discuss what rejecting his ministry would look like.

1. Which best explains how you like to learn (circle two)?

Reading books	Listening to teachers
Group discussion	Stories
Pictures/visual	Hands on
Television/movies	Friends

2. Imagine you're giving a speech at school on how students should act in the cafeteria at lunch. List two or three reasons why using stories might be better than a PowerPoint presentation.

3. Get with two or three others and read each of the following parables Jesus told. What is the illustration used and the main point of each one?

	ILLUSTRATION	MAIN POINT
Matthew 13:44		
Luke 6:43-45		
Luke 12:35-40		

4. Read Mark 4:13 and then Matthew 13:10-13. Why were the disciples frustrated?

5. Complete these sentences:

My relationship to God is like he's a _____ because _____.
                          (relationship)

Being at school is like _____ because I _____.
                    (a job or profession)

It's ironic, really, because I say I _____, but when I get the
                          (state a goal that you have)

chance, I act like a _____ because _____.
                (animal or person)

THIS WEEK

Contemporary culture is a culture of story—we engage with stories in movies, on television, and in books. We even have video games with storylines in which participants assume a role and identity. In an age of mass media, Jesus' use of parables as a teaching method should connect well with students. This TalkSheet is an upbeat lesson that teaches students about Jesus' use of parables.

OPENER

Before the meeting, create some modern-day parables, leaving blanks for students to fill in. Work with your group to write a parable or two. Feel free to create your own, too. As students come to each blank, they're to write a word or phrase based on the prompts in parentheses. See if you can construct a good parable or two as a group. The following is an example you can write on the whiteboard or pass out on paper.

EXAMPLE: When a person (write an activity or select one of these—wakes up in the morning/argues with parents), she can be like a (animal or occupation) that (what the animal/occupation does). The (animal/occupation) will (activity that animal/occupation does that helps us understand better). So, listen to me when I say that you should (provide a sentence that teaches others what they should learn from this). If you don't, you'll be like the (an animal/occupation opposite of what you're teaching), which (give an example of why she's an opposite).

DISCUSSION

1. How do your students like to learn? Ask students to report which ones they circled and write the totals on the board. What does this say about how we learn? How do teachers at school teach? How does church or youth group teaching take place? Should we change how we teach to match how most people learn?

2. What are some of the reasons a story might work better than other teaching techniques? What could the problems be with a story? Could you teach as much information in a story as with another method? Is information as important?

3. Let students report what they wrote down as the illustration and the main points. When they're fin-ished, ask students to look over the main points. What did Jesus want his listeners to understand? Did any parents have stories from their childhoods that they told regularly to teach a point? Have students share some of the better ones.

4. Have your students ever been frustrated with a teacher who was difficult to understand? What was it like to be in that teacher's class? What could the teacher have done to communicate better? What do you think the disciples wanted? Can you relate to this frustration? What was Jesus' frustration with the disciples?

5. What symbols do your students have in their bedrooms at home? On their cars, notebooks, or lockers? What do these symbols represent? What did your students notice about trying to use words as symbols for their relationship with God, their approach to school, and their goals in life?

CLOSE

Sum up the lesson by encouraging students to do a parable hunt and read some of the parables of Jesus this week in Matthew, Mark, and Luke. Provide a list of references for your students. Encourage students to be aware to whom Jesus directed the parable, the context, the setting, the main point, and any explanations following it.

MORE

• In Matthew 13, Jesus begins to teach in parables after being rejected in Jerusalem by the Pharisees. Though there's some debate about how to interpret this, it seems that he wanted to communicate to those who were able to understand (verse 16) and keep the meaning from unbelievers (verses 13-15). Is it difficult for visitors to your group to understand certain words, lessons, or songs? How might using stories or parables help the group communicate better with visitors? Divide your group into equal teams and have them come up with five ideas for good stories that illustrate key topics.

• Parables use some symbolic language in the form of irony, metaphor, analogy, or simile. These are common features in popular songs, wise sayings, poetry, and movies. A quick Internet search can help you locate Web sites that give examples. Locate 10 popular examples of metaphors and make a handout students can use to connect the symbolic language with its meaning. Why do singers and writers use symbolic language versus just saying something in a straightforward manner? Is our culture heading toward symbolism or away from it? Why or why not?

1. At the time of Jesus' teaching, the smallest everyday item people were familiar with was a mustard seed. Write down the two smallest items you can think of. After you're done, use them as examples to complete this sentence: "Life is like a _____ because" and then give an example of how life can be like those objects.

2. In what area of your life have you seen the most growth: (1) Over the past two years? (2) Since you were a child? Write down as many examples of growth as you can identify:

3. Read Mark 4:26-32. Jesus' main teaching topic was about the kingdom of God. Different from a political kingdom, this was and is a spiritual kingdom with Jesus at the center. Look up the following verses and write down what each says about the kingdom of God.

Mark 1:15

Mark 10:14-16

Romans 14:17

4. Look through this list of ways that the kingdom of God grows. Put a checkmark next to the three you want to do best.

___ Being a good example in following Christ.
___ Obeying what the Bible says.
___ Giving my time to help the poor or needy.
___ Standing up for the outcasts at school.
___ Praying that God will use me to help others.

___ Serving others without notice.
___ Sharing my faith through words.
___ Trying to reach my friends for Christ.
___ Being an advocate for children.
___ Growing a heart for missions to the world.

5. Look around the room and really see the people around you. Realize that Jesus Christ is present and the kingdom of God is here now. Imagine that as you leave today, you're being planted in the world to grow the kingdom through your actions and words. Write down two specific actions you can take this week to help grow God's kingdom:

THIS WEEK

From the very beginning of his public ministry, Jesus spoke about the kingdom of God. This theological concept is important when thinking about what it means to be the church (or part of the church) within today's culture. Students need to understand that the kingdom of God is a present reality that affects how they live out their faith each week. This lesson uses two parables to introduce students to what Jesus meant by the "kingdom of God," and then apply it to their lives.

OPENING

Announce you're going to play a rousing game of "The Expert's Club" and select three of the best exaggerators who can bluff through what they're talking about even when they have no clue! Look for volunteers, but select from among them the three who will do the best job up front. Bring the three up front and tell the group that each person is going to have two minutes (no more!) to explain how a seed grows. The group will vote on who did the best job at appearing expert, and the winner gets a fabulous prize from you.

When you're done, transition into the lesson by telling them that no one knows how a seed knows to grow, it just does. In the same way, Jesus taught that the kingdom of God is like a tiny seed that grows into a very large plant. Tell students that the kingdom of God was an important subject in Jesus' teaching and is the focus of this TalkSheet.

DISCUSSION

1. You should be having fun after the opening, and you'll want to keep the fun rolling on this one. After a few minutes, ask if anyone has one that's really funny. Allow anyone who wants to share their particularly funny ones. If time permits, quickly ask if anyone had one they could share that they thought was especially insightful, but make sure you've got different students sharing on this second one.
2. People experience growth in multiple ways—physically, socially, mentally, and spiritually (Luke 2:52). We also grow in ways that aren't so obvious, like our experiences and our perspectives. Ask students for examples of how they've grown through their experiences. Ask them how their perspective is different from when they were a kid. In what ways do they see the world differently, cope with problems more effectively, or live more aware of others?

3. What did the students write down for the verses about the kingdom of God? If students are interested in more verses on the subject, have them look at Colossians 1:13-14; Hebrews 12:28; and Revelation 1:6.
4. It's easy to emphasize one aspect of the kingdom of God over another when teaching it to students. Some see the kingdom as an inward and personal reality that connects to the future kingdom, while others emphasize the active, real-life side of the kingdom of God. This list incorporates both, modeling the balanced ideal that the kingdom is a spiritual reality that requires us to serve the hurting and outcast as Jesus did. Discuss with students the implications for their lives. Does this change anything for them?
5. Tell students that the kingdom of God is in their community. It's a present reality as the reign of God spreads among people, and relevant since it's not just about the future but about the now. Challenge the students to live by faith, trusting that the King is also their heavenly Father who asks us to participate in the mission and purpose of the kingdom. You may want to reread Luke 4:43.

CLOSING

Close by having a prayer time for your group. Remind students that the kingdom of God is a spiritual kingdom centering on Jesus Christ and his power. So prayer is integral since it's to be a kingdom built on his spirit and not our might (Zechariah 4:6). Have a time of silent prayer so students can pray for opportunities to put their answers to question #5 into practice this week. After a minute or so, a leader can close with a prayer for the group.

MORE

• **The mustard seed was about half the size of the head of a pin and would produce an herb plant that would grow 10 to 12 feet high. Find a short video on the Internet that shows, in stop action, a seed growing. There are quite a few online—search for "seed sprouting" on YouTube.com or Google.com.**

• **Have students read Luke 4:43, where Jesus declares he was sent specifically to preach the "good news" of the kingdom of God. The people of that day confused his message with their hope for a political kingdom (Daniel 2:44; Matthew 5:19-20; Mark 10:35-45; Luke 8:1; John 6:15; Acts 1:6; Romans 14:15; Revelation 19:11-16).**

1. What is your favorite meal? Construct an ideal meal by circling one item in each line below:

First course: Tossed salad   Coleslaw   Cornbread   Fresh fruit   Soup

Veggie: Corn   Green beans   Peas   Asparagus   Carrots

Starch: Fries   Baked potato   Rice   Rolls   Crackers

Main: More veggies   Chicken   Fish   Steak   Pizza

Drink: Pepsi/Coke   Sprite   Mountain Dew   Milk   Fresh juice

Dessert: Cake   Fruit pie   Ice cream   Chocolate   Custard

JESUS PROVIDES
The feeding of the 5,000
(John 6:5-15)

2. Read through the story again. Describe what Philip was thinking:

What do you think Andrew's perspective was?

3. Jesus asks Philip, "Where shall we buy bread for these people to eat?" Put a check next to which of the following best explains why Jesus tests Philip with this question.

____ Jesus didn't know how to feed them.

____ Since Philip was from Bethsaida, a nearby town, he knew where to get food.

____ Jesus wanted to show that it was not possible to do this by human effort.

____ Jesus was testing Philip to see if Philip knew that only through God could this be done.

4. What do you do when you're facing a big task or responsibility with a lot of pressure? For each one below, put a Y for "That's like me," an N for "That's not like me," or a D for "It depends on the situation."

____ I get busy and distracted with something else and end up putting off what I need to do.

____ I ignore the issue and hope it will go away.

____ I delay doing it and watch TV, play video games, get online, or spend time with friends.

____ I try to get someone else to do it for me or help me with it.

____ I usually think I can't do it or do it well, so I have a hard time caring.

____ I'm usually overwhelmed—big tasks feel too big to me.

____ I work through it step by step until it gets done.

____ I like challenges.

____ I pray about it before taking it on.

____ I pray about it when things get difficult.

5. This story shows Christ's compassion and his ability to provide. Identify ways you can rely more on God and think less about doing things in your own strength this week.

From *High School TalkSheets: 50 Ready-to-Use Discussions on the Life of Christ* by Terry Linhart. Permission to reproduce this page granted only for use in buyer's youth group. Copyright © 2009 by Youth Specialties. www.youthspecialties.com

THIS WEEK

One of the most familiar of Jesus' miracles, the feeding of the 5,000 shows Jesus' great love and provision for people. This TalkSheet connects students' lives with the reality that God is their provider and helps them think about what that looks like in their lives.

OPENER

One of the best ways to bring life to familiar stories is to help students experience what it was like to be there. Before the meeting, set a small table covered with a cloth somewhere up front. Place paper bowls of food containing pieces of bread, cheese, and bologna behind the table. Arrange to have several students play disciples. Be as creative as you want. To reenact the scene, encourage students to come to your meeting a bit hungry by skipping the previous meal. Have two different people read the passage back-to-back as students reflect on it and, during this reflection, send the disciples to fetch the food from behind the table and serve it to the rest of the students. When done, ask students to imagine what it must have been like to have food provided for them. What would it have been like to see such a large crowd fed in such a way?

DISCUSSION

1. Have students share their meal selections. What was the most common meal choice for your group? Did anyone pick asparagus or something else unusual? What wasn't on the menu that your students like?
2. This is the only miracle besides the resurrection that's in all four Gospels. Why is this a significant event? What does it say about who Jesus is? Ask students what they think the disciples were thinking during this event. Philip and Andrew are specifically mentioned—what are their concerns?
3. Philip was from a nearby town, so it made sense that Jesus asked him instead of the others. John writes in verse 6 that this was a test, but it also showed that lunch wasn't going to happen though human effort—a testimony of God's ability to provide. How does God want to be the provider in the lives of people today? How many days during this past week were the students conscious of God as their provider?
4. What did your kids notice while working through these? Which one was the hardest to be honest about? What role did God's ability to provide play in how they decided to answer? If God were answering these for them, which answer(s) would he want to change? Ask some students to give examples of moments when they handled a large responsibility well. No one will ever get rid of all pressure or responsibility, but they can choose how they respond to those moments.
5. Encourage your students to think about how they start their day each morning. Do they focus on just getting through the day, or on how much they can get out of the day? What if they started each morning by committing the day to God and then trusting him as they walked through the day?

CLOSE

It's easy to see challenging situations through human eyes—measuring how they'll be solved by filtering them through our own experiences and understanding, and by viewing them in the light of our own worries and fears. What if God wanted to do something amazing in our lives? How would we know? Would we trust him enough to let him use us? What would it take for us to be willing to allow the same Jesus who fed over 5,000 people lead us and provide for us? What makes this difficult for so many? How is the John 6:5 story different from ours? How is it similar?

MORE

A variation on the opener would be to fix up a table ahead of time with a hole in the top and a sheet over the table, cutting a flap in it where the hole would be. Place a student under the table beforehand with some pizza slices. Reenact the scene from the Bible story, but contemporize it—have the "little boy" carry a pizza instead of fish and bread. Have the "disciples" bring the "kid" and a prepped pizza box to the front. Place the prepped box of pizza over the hole and lift up the lid so it blocks the students' view. (The pizza box should have the bottom pre-cut so the leader can have additional pizza slices handed up by the person under the table.) The effect should be that many pizza slices come out of the table and provide enough pizza for all. Students will eventually figure it out, of course, and this provides a great opportunity for discussion. Remind students that what Jesus did was a true miracle, not a trick—look at what the crowd of over 5,000 wanted to do with Christ (verse 15).

1. On this scale, rate how strong your faith in Christ is by drawing a stick figure on the line.

◀ • ▶

1 (weakest)   (strongest) 10

2. Describe the worst storm you've ever seen or experienced.

What feelings did you have when you saw it?

3. Read Matthew 14:25-33. Write a one-sentence headline summarizing what happened in this scene.

4. You're in a small boat full of people. The wind is howling and the boat is swaying violently from side to side. What are you thinking? Do you panic?

If you then saw a man in the distance on the water, how would you react? Would you be more afraid or less afraid?

5. Do you A (agree) or D (disagree)?

_____ The men on the boat were frightened.
_____ Peter could've walked on the water without the presence of Jesus.
_____ Peter let his fear of his surroundings get in the way of his faith in Christ.
_____ If given the chance, you'd be able to step out of the boat and walk.

6. In the story, Peter sank because he was afraid and took his eyes off of Jesus. Yet even though Peter let fear overtake him, Jesus was still there to lift him out of the waters and calm the stormy winds. Are there areas of your life where you've taken your eyes off Jesus? Is there an area where you've taken steps toward Jesus, but feel like you're sinking and need God to lift you up and calm the storms? Write down any area that comes to mind and silently pray that God will lift you up as you place your faith in him.

THIS WEEK

The Bible states that we're saved by faith. A dramatic moment when these steps of faith were illustrated was when Peter walked on the water toward Christ. This TalkSheet will assist those who feel they have, like Peter, taken steps toward God only to find they're afraid or sinking and in need of God to lift them up.

OPENER

This is a great lesson in which to use the classic Trust Fall. This activity is designed to test the trust and faith of the group members in each other. (You may want to consider only asking for willing participants versus pressuring everyone to do this). In this activity one person stands on an object slightly higher than waist level. The students on the floor stand facing one another in two lines holding hands firmly with the person across from them. Station another person at the end of each line to support the head of the person who's falling. Have the falling person face away from the group and stand with arms crossed over his or her chest. When the group is ready and secure, the person will fall backward into the group's hands, or at least try to, depending on the amount of faith the falling person has in the rest of the group.

After everyone who has chosen to participate has had a turn, gather the whole group together and discuss how they felt while they trusted their peers to catch them. Ask how it felt to feel helpless yet still fall into their peers' hands, relying only on their faith in their peers? Was everyone successful? Did someone not make it? Make sure no comments are made toward someone who chose not to do this activity or didn't do it "right."

DISCUSSION

1. What factors did students consider in rating themselves? How many rated themselves 5 or higher on the scale (have them raise their hands)? Is it easier to assess oneself higher or lower?
2. Have students share their storm stories. This will take some time, so set a time limit for sharing for each student. Enable as many students to share as possible.
3. What headlines did your students come up with?

4. Discuss with the students their answers for this situation. Why did Peter want to walk on the water? Ask how many would have even thought to want to walk on the water toward Jesus. Is the point of the story that they should've wanted to do that?
5. Ask the students which statements they agreed with or disagreed with. Why did they feel this way?
6. This would be a great opportunity to share a story from your own life that connects to the themes of the story.

CLOSE

So, what's the moral of the story? Discuss with your students what they think it is. Peter had the faith to get out of the boat, but then doubted (Matthew 28:17). Despite that, he's the one who serves as the model for taking faith steps. Remind students that we may desire to follow Christ, but that sometimes we'll find ourselves doubting or sinking. Have students review their answers for question #6 and then listen as you read the prayer in Psalm 144:7-9: "Reach down your hand from on high; deliver me and rescue me from the mighty waters, from the hands of foreigners whose mouths are full of lies, whose right hands are deceitful. I will sing a new song to you, my God."

MORE

• **You may want to show a short storm video downloaded online or borrowed from your local library. Use it to kick off your lesson or to talk with your students about storms. How often do storms come along? What effect do storms have on our lives—do we get more fearful or do we realize that God is in charge and that whatever happens is under his control?**
• **For more on faith, have students read James 2:14-26 to discuss the role of faith and actions, particularly in light of what Peter did. Romans 4:18-25 shows how Abraham acted in faith, a key passage in Hebrews 11.**

(Thanks to Danno Lambert for the TalkSheet idea)

1. For each line below, circle the choice that best defines who you are.

Football, Tennis, Swimming, Basketball, Baseball, Auto Racing

Beach, Mall, Ski Slope, Swimming Pool, Garage, Woods, Field

iPod, mp3, email, blogs, DVD, IM

Hip-hop, Jazz, Country, Electronica, Pop, Alternative, Christian

New York, Florida, Chicago, San Diego, Vancouver, Denver

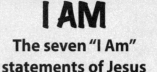

I AM

The seven "I Am" statements of Jesus

(John 6:35; 8:12; 10:7-9, 11-14; 11:25-26; 14:6; 15:1, 5)

2. Pick at least four of the following verses and fill in the words Jesus uses to describe himself. Then give your perspective on what each means.

VERSE	WHAT JESUS IS	WHAT IT MEANS
John 6:35		
John 8:12		
John 10:7-9		
John 10:11-14		
John 11:25		
John 14:6		
John 15:5		

3. Pick two of the "I am" statements you think best show who Jesus is. How would you explain that to others? For each of these two, write a sentence that a seven-year-old kid could understand.

4. Imagine that Jesus wanted to remind you of who he is. What might he say? Fill in the blanks below with some possible answers.

I am the _____ for you, so that you can _____.

I am your _____, because you need me to _____.

THIS WEEK

Jesus was more than just a prophet or a great moral teacher. His listeners understood clearly that Jesus claimed to be God. We see this understanding develop as we see how Jesus reveals more about who he is. In this TalkSheet lesson, your students will encounter Jesus'"I am" statements and apply them to their lives.

OPENER

Find the movie *The Gospel of John* and show the scene from the end of John 8 where Jesus is teaching the people about who he is. The clip should end just after the narrator reports that Jesus disappeared. What do your students notice about this scene? What was Jesus saying when he said, "I am"? What did the people understand that Jesus was claiming? Read Exodus 3:14 and Philippians 2:6. Jesus made specific claims about who he was. Today we're going to look at those claims and discuss how they affect our lives today.

DISCUSSION

1. Have students get in groups of four and share their answers. How do words like this help people know more about us? How are they limited in describing who we are?

2. Have the groups talk about their answers. They can fill in any boxes with answers from others for lines they didn't complete. Have a copy on an overhead or whiteboard and ask students to share their answers. Record answers in the boxes on the overhead. Which of these were new to your students? Which make the most sense? Which are unclear?

   Bread of life—spiritual sustenance, not from external sources in this world, but from Jesus.
   Light of the world—shows us the correct path. For more, see 1 John 1:6-7.
   The gate/door—only through Jesus can we have spiritual sanctuary or salvation.
   The Good Shepherd—he cares for and protects the flock. See Isaiah 40:11.
   The resurrection and life—Jesus gives eternal life. See John 5:24 and 10:28.

The way, truth, and life—salvation is not through many ways, but through Christ alone.
The vine—we are to be connected and bear fruit.

3. It's often hard to explain spiritual concepts to children, but it's helpful in getting students to think about the "so what?" factor. Ask students to share what they wrote. Some will have done this well and others will have struggled. Let students volunteer to share.

4. Have your students think over the "I am" statements Jesus made. Why can Jesus make these statements? Why did Jesus use word pictures to communicate deep truths? Encourage them to look over their responses. Do you think God still wants to communicate with people in relevant ways? How does he do that? What is our role in that process?

CLOSE

It's easy to get in a routine and lose sight of who Jesus said he was. These statements show Jesus' place as the central figure in history. More than a historical figure, though, Jesus, through his "I am" statements, reveals himself as relational, not impersonal. Encourage students to look over the different statements and think of ways each one has been true in their lives.

MORE

• **Faith is a key part of life. To be a Christian means putting faith in Christ. How does not believing in God also require faith? What beliefs would that involve? What type of faith response does each of the "I am" statements require of Jesus' listeners?**

• **Is faith a blind step or a step made based on knowledge? Does it take faith to believe Abraham Lincoln existed? That men walked on the moon? That Jesus is who he says he is? Ask students, "On what do people base their beliefs?"**

• **List their answers on the board. The answers could include: Prior experience or observations, parents, documents, artifacts, tradition, culture, being an eyewitness. Ask students which ones are the most convincing the them.**

1. Imagine you've been chosen as the new principal of your school. What two or three rules would you make or change?

What if you were the President of the United States? What's the first thing you'd change?

2. Read John 6:60. What was the complaint of some of his disciples?

What did they do (verse 66)?

3. Read verses 51, 54, and 55. What does Jesus mean by the bread and blood?

Do you think these disciples misunderstood what Jesus was saying? Why or why not?

4. Read verse 63, then read 1 Corinthians 2:14-15. Write down one or two ways people gain spiritual understanding and why people sometimes don't understand.

5. When do you most feel like giving up on something? Put an arrow next to the reasons that best describe these moments.

When I'm tired	When I disagree	When I'm overwhelmed
When things are unfair	When there's too much work	When I'm not confident
When there won't be any results	When I don't know what to do	When no one will care

THIS WEEK

As Jesus' followers began to understand his teaching, some didn't like what they were hearing. Some people who came face-to-face with Jesus and saw him do many miracles and even became his disciples walked away from him. It should come as no surprise today that some who hear about Jesus and experience his love still turn and walk away. This TalkSheet explores the tension between responding to Jesus' invitation and trying to please the crowd.

OPENER

Tell students you think there's room for a new political party for their country. It needs to be a very popular group with themes most people will like. Ask what campaign topics they should address to make this as popular as possible. Write the answers on the board—make sure your students are really thinking about this. What do they think would actually work? When finished, ask students if these are workable or outrageous. Try to work with your students to focus on three or four main themes from this list that would be compelling issues for a new party. Finish by asking your students if politicians should work to be popular. How about church leaders? With whom was Jesus popular? Unpopular? Today's scene shows that even some of those who followed Jesus and were called his disciples deserted Jesus.

DISCUSSION

1. Have fun with this one. Have students share their answers. When you get some funny or insightful ones, ask others what would happen if they were put into action. Which of your students' answers focused on doing what was popular, and which ones showed good leadership, even though they wouldn't necessarily be well received?

2. Ask your students about what people in the church today choose to complain about. Do adults complain about different things than teenagers? Should people complain about church issues?

3. What do your students think Jesus meant in verses 53-58? Did the disciples who left choose to walk away even though they understood his words, or were they confused? What does it mean that these people were called disciples in addition to the 12? Jesus came down from heaven and preached a message about his coming death and sacrifice, symbolized by the bread and blood. Some followed Jesus for political reasons, thinking he was going to overthrow the Romans. When he started to talk of his death and a spiritual kingdom, those people walked away. What are some reasons people walk away from Jesus today?

4. Have students share their answers. Ask them if they understand what Paul says in 1 Corinthians. Does it mean that if a lifelong Christian sitting in church can't understand the sermon, she should be concerned about whether she's a Christian then? Feel free to clarify any confusion—the word *accept* here indicates a hostility toward the message of God (Romans 8:7).

5. Would your teens say society hangs in there through difficult times, or do people quit when things get tough? Did any of your students once take music lessons (or any other lessons) but later quit? How do they feel now about having quit? What are some remedies to help them through times when they feel like quitting?

CLOSE

Summarize by reminding students there are two issues. First, Jesus' message demands a response from his listeners or followers. Second, the example of the disciples who turned away provides a challenge for us as we consider our own faithfulness to Christ. What would cause us to want to turn away? Ask students to close their eyes, then read John 12:25-26: "Those who love their life will lose it, while those who hate their life in this world will keep it for eternal life. Whoever serves me must follow me; and where I am, my servant also will be. My Father will honor the one who serves me." Ask students to reflect on their lives right now and evaluate their response to God's leading in their lives. Do they find themselves resisting God's direction, or are they willing to follow Christ wherever he may lead them? Allow them some time, maybe play a relevant song and have them write about this, and close with prayer.

MORE

• **Complaining and grumbling have been a part of dealing with people since the early days of Genesis. It is rarely beneficial, yet some of us, even leaders, engage in it frequently. You may want to explore some passages that discuss the topic, such as Numbers 14:26-37; Psalm 78:17-21; 1 Corinthians 10:6-10; Philippians 2:12-18; 2 Timothy 2:22-26; and James 5:7-11. What implications are present in these verses? Can we really learn to not complain, grumble, or argue? What should our goal be, based on these verses?**

• **Quitting. Most adults would say people are more prone to quitting than they used to be. There may be some truth in that, but it's a common human problem. Set up the lesson by exploring quitting. It won't be too difficult to find stories of celebrities and sports figures who quit on sports teams, marriages, or contracts. Bring those examples to your meeting. Have students read them and then discuss whether it was okay for the person to quit. How do your students determine when it's okay to quit something? When is it not acceptable?**

1. Who do people say Jesus is? Check all the definitions you've heard people say:

____ A prophet
____ A man who is "just all right with me"
____ The Son of God
____ A made-up person
____ Savior and Lord
____ A great moral teacher
____ One of many gods
____ Too confusing to think about
____ The Son of Man
____ An example of how we should live

"YOU ARE THE CHRIST!"

Peter's confession

(Matthew 16:13-19)

2. Read verse 14. What "job" do these people have in common?

How is Jesus different from them?

3. What is significant about Peter's response? Define these terms from verse 16:

Messiah -

Son of the living God -

4. Below is a list of important functions in the church. Circle the ones that are meaningful to you. Put a checkmark next to the ones that are important, but not meaningful to you. Leave the rest blank.

Teaching/preaching	Group prayer	Being with other Christians
Communion or Eucharist	Worship through music	Baptism
Potluck dinners	Liturgy	Mission trips/service projects
Retreats/camps	Dramas/musicals	Giving/tithing
Support missions	Community involvement	Traditional music
Bible study	Small groups	Other _____

5. How has the teaching ministry of the church helped you grow in your faith? For each of the following, give a grade (A, B, C, D, or F) for how well the church has helped you learn and grow in these areas:

Understanding the Bible _____

How to share my faith _____

How to obey God _____

How to handle my problems _____

Knowing more about who Jesus is _____

Understanding who the Holy Spirit is _____

How to reach out to others _____

How to grow in my relationship with Jesus _____

THIS WEEK

Pop quizzes. We don't know when they're coming, but they show how much we really know—or don't know. Jesus gave his disciples a pop quiz about who he was. Many in Jesus' time were trying to figure out who he was, and the disciples were no different. Sometimes they understood, and other times they missed the mark. Peter aced the quiz, and Jesus responded with the profound declarations that are the focus of this TalkSheet.

OPENER

Make a handout of 10 trivia questions. Get two or three from contemporary news headlines of the week, two or three from a Bible trivia Web page, and three or four historical questions found online. Divide your group into four equal groups and tell them you're going to give them a trivia pop quiz. Pass out the handout to each group and give them three minutes to fill in the answers. Next, give correct answers, asking them to grade their own, and give a small prize to the winning group. Ask students how they keep up with all the information that's out there. Is there such a thing as information overload? How do they determine which information is true? What are we supposed to do with all the information we can find on the Internet?

DISCUSSION

1. At a key point in history, Jesus came to earth and backed up his claims to be God with miracles, powerful teaching, and uncommon love. Discover which of the answers your group found to be the most prominent. In what ways could these answers cause people to doubt?

2. Jesus' message was prophetic, so people tried to discern if Jesus was truly a prophet. He was more than a prophet, however—he was Immanuel, "God with us," a fulfillment of the prophecies. This was difficult for many to accept in Jesus' day. Brainstorm with your students a list of objections their friends have for accepting who Jesus is today. Then go a step further and help them identify what types of objections these are (e.g., intellectual, moral, theological).

3. Peter said something like this before (John 6:69). What did Peter mean by *Messiah*? Have students check out verses 21-23. Why do you think Peter

didn't understand Jesus' plan? What does "Son of the living God" imply? How is that different from the prophets' claims?

4. Jesus said he would build his church on Peter's commitment. What does he mean by church? What is the purpose of the church? What should be the purpose of the church? Does Acts 2:42 give any helpful hints?

5. Refer students to verse 19. The person who held the keys controlled who entered or didn't enter a home. In the same way, Jesus says that the church (us) is the way people will hear about, and be able to enter, the kingdom of God (read Matthew 23:13 for an illustration of the opposite). How did your students learn how to obey God? How to handle problems? How to interpret moral problems that their culture presents? What grades did your students give their church? What surprises were there for you?

CLOSE

Remind your students that the church is not a man-made institution, but something Christ himself created. What authority does the church have in the lives of people? What authority should it have? Do some church denominations have more authority than others? What should our commitment be to a local church?

MORE

• **If you want to add to the lesson, take a video camera out and do on-the-street interviews, asking people who Jesus is. Edit together the better answers and show a three-to-four-minute video from that. You'll have better quality if you use a camera and a handheld microphone rather than relying on the camera's microphone. Try to select an area where you can conduct the interviews without problems and where you'll get a wide variety of answers from mostly local people.**

• **Do most people in churches today understand most of the words and phrases pastors and others use? Ask students if there are concepts or phrases that are regularly talked about in churches that they don't understand. You may want to pass out slips of paper and have students write them down. You can then answer some of them, create an online Wiki for your group, or devote a whole meeting to it.**

1. What have been the highlights of your life? Under each category, fill in the two or three greatest moments.

MY SOCIAL LIFE   MY ACTIVE LIFE   MY SPIRITUAL LIFE

MOUNTAINTOP SURPRISE

The transfiguration

(Mark 9:2-10)

2. Read Mark 9:2-5. Which of the following best describes Peter's response?

___ He was really scared and didn't know what to do, but he had to say something.

___ He wanted to stay there and keep the wonderful experience going.

___ He thought Christ's kingdom had come and that therefore three tabernacles were needed.

3. If you were called on at school to write a sentence introducing Jesus to the world, what would you say? Write it down.

If you wrote a sentence introducing Jesus to your church, what would that sentence say?

Were your two sentences similar or different? Why or why not?

4. Read Mark 9:7-9. The voice of God said to "listen to Him." What does that mean?

5. Imagine you're walking off the mountain with the three disciples. What thoughts were going through their minds? Write down as many as you can think of.

THIS WEEK

The Christian life can be a journey of highs and lows, of mountaintop experiences and deep valleys of uncertainty—a challenge to our ability to stay consistent. It's sometimes more difficult to maintain a consistent relationship with God when things are going well. This lesson uses the transfiguration of Christ to help students discuss these ups and downs in their Christian journey.

OPENER

To start the discussion, have a fast-paced brainstorming discussion on the topic of feeling close to God. Tell students that youth leaders sometimes hear people say, "I don't feel like I have a close relationship with God." What do they mean by this? Have any of your students said this before? What do they mean by the word "feel"? Does it mean they've been cut off from God? Can a person sense (or feel) whether their relationship with God is close or not? What is the danger in relying on our feelings to determine how we're doing?

DISCUSSION

1. Were any highlights easier to come up with than others? Have a few students volunteer their answers. Are they quick to share one column over another? (Make sure to specifically ask for answers from the "my spiritual life" column if you don't hear any.) Explain that some people call these mountaintop experiences, a phrase that comes from the story we're looking at today in Mark 9:2-10.
2. Peter, though not asked, felt that he had to say something. Have students ever had incredible spiritual experiences that they wanted to extend? Can people be scared even when they're having an amazing spiritual experience with God? Remind students that Christ's transfiguration was a change into another form—the way he'll appear when he comes a second time. Why would that produce fear in the disciples?
3. Let your students share their sentences. What was the focus of their introductions? Keep track of this and briefly summarize those observations before moving to #4. Did they use the same introductions for the two groups, or did they change them?
4. The phrase means "be obedient to Him" (and connects to Deuteronomy 18:15). Why do you think God chooses to say this? What did your students write down in their introductory sentences? Did any of them have something about obedience? Why is obedience a big deal to God when it usually isn't as prominent in our thinking of God?
5. Have students share what they wrote. Jesus shared about his coming death and resurrection, which caused confusion among the disciples. Why did Jesus want them to keep this silent until later? How did the disciples feel about having to come down from the mountain? Why did they have to come down from the mountain? Have you ever had a similar moment coming back from a camp, retreat, or short-term mission trip?

CLOSE

How does a mountaintop experience with God transform our lives? Can we have a strong relationship with God without having mountaintop experiences? How can they be harmful to a relationship with God? Have students reflect on the spiritual highlights in their lives. Were these moments connected to planned events, or did they just happen? Close by discussing ways your group can make themselves available for God to do transformational things.

MORE

• **Peter actually reflects about this experience in 1 Peter 1:12-21. As you read through this, describe what role this mountaintop experience played in Peter's life. What confidence did it give him? How does he use the experience to both encourage and challenge his readers?**
• **The same reflections Peter gives his readers in 1 Peter can be found by holding a panel discussion with older Christian adults—no more than three—who can share their experiences. Ask them to talk about their mountaintop experiences and how these experiences contributed to their faith in God. What role did those, and the low times, play in their lives? Keep the panel discussion moving and coach your participants to keep their answers concise.**

1. **What are you most like during conflict and similar moments where forgiveness is needed?**

____ Judge: I assign penalties to people who wrong me and make them pay.

____ Time bomb: I hold a grudge inside for now and explode later.

____ Scorekeeper: I keep a record of how people treat me and I know the score.

____ Duck: Stuff that happens to me rolls off my back and I stay afloat.

____ Hugger: I try to avoid conflict, so I forgive quickly.

FORGIVE? FORGET IT!
The unmerciful servant
(Matthew 18:21-35)

2. **For each of the following, give your best guess:**

Times a week the average high school student gets angry: _____

Percent of high school students who are regularly bitter about something: ____

Percent of people who believe anger will just go away if it's ignored: _____

3. **Read Matthew 18:21. What do you think Peter is really asking Jesus?**

Based on Job 33:29-30 and Amos 1:3, how many times did people of that day think they were required to forgive?

4. **Read over Matthew 18:23-30. Which of the following best explains why the first servant wasn't willing to forgive the second servant who owed him so little?**

____ He wasn't truly grateful for being forgiven himself.

____ He was greedy (which was why he owed so much), and greed drove his refusal to forgive.

____ He just worked for the master—he didn't want to be like him.

____ His angry personality just got the best of him.

5. **Look at these two verses and rewrite them so they describe true forgiveness.**

Colossians 3:13—

Ephesians 4:32—

THIS WEEK

Some conflict in life is unavoidable. So are moments when we disobey God. The issue isn't whether they happen, it's how we respond to them. Anger, bitterness, sarcasm (simmering anger), and envy seem all too common today, even in youth groups and churches. This TalkSheet provides ample opportunity to discuss forgiveness, but the real goal is to get students to implement what they already know about forgiveness. Read the story before students begin their TalkSheets.

OPENER

Ask students to think of a time they behaved badly or made a big mistake, but were forgiven for it. Ask students not to share the specific details. Ask them what it felt like to be in a situation where they did something wrong, but were forgiven. Did other people truly forgive them? How did they know? Do people forgive more easily today than they did when your parents were kids? Why or why not? Remind students that we're all in need of forgiveness, and that part of Jesus' mission to earth was to offer—and model—God's forgiveness for sin.

DISCUSSION

1. Divide your students into five groups. Have them go to the group representing their answer. Have the students in each group discuss why they chose that description. Let them talk for about five minutes and then draw their attention back to you. Have students brainstorm reasons why people react to conflict in different ways. Take note of which group was the largest and which was the smallest. Then let students return to their original spots.

2. Have students share their answers to these three, but go through them one at a time to see if there's a consensus among your students. Would your students say there's a lot of anger and hurt within most teens today? Is it different for adults? It's important to let your students know that anger that isn't dealt with won't go away by itself. What does this say for those who bottle up their feelings?

3. Is there a limit to how many times your students should have to forgive someone else? Is there ever a situation where they don't have to forgive someone else? In what situations is it the hardest for people to forgive someone else? You may have opportunity to discuss how envy and jealousy contribute to people's unwillingness to forgive.

4. The larger sum of money was equal to well over $12 million today. The smaller amount was about $20. Which of the reasons listed did your students select? How are these four similar to reasons why people don't forgive others?

5. How did your students describe what forgiveness is? What reason do these references give for why we must forgive?

CLOSE

Most people are quite aware of Jesus' teaching on forgiveness. The trick isn't to have a good discussion about it, as you have done today, but rather to put it into practice in everyday life. What keeps people from putting forgiveness into practice? What are the barriers to forgiveness? Is forgiveness an important part of being like Jesus?

MORE

• **This lesson would make a good one for a melodrama as an introduction. Find three students with dramatic flair. Read the story and have them act it out, repeating the quotes after you read them. You'll need a couple of extra people to be the other servants. When finished, ask students what they noticed in the story.**

• **Find a TV show with a scene on forgiveness. After showing the scene(s), ask students how realistic it was. What issue needed forgiveness? What factors kept forgiveness from being easy?**

• **For more on God as the God of forgiveness, have students connect with these verses: Nehemiah 9:17; Psalm 103:12; Isaiah 43:25; and Jeremiah 31:34. Writers note that the teaching of the day was to forgive someone three times. It's possible Peter got the notion of "seven" from Proverbs 24:16 and Amos 2:1.**

1. Complete the following sentences:

A salesperson is someone who…

A missionary is someone who…

THE FIRST SHORT-TERM MISSIONS TRIP
The 72 are sent out and return
(Luke 10:1-12; 17-22)

2. Short-term mission trips are common in youth groups. Write out a definition for "mission."

3. Read Luke 10:2.

Who are the workers?

What's the harvest field?

4. Look over verses 4-10. What message were they preaching?

5. Read verses 17-22. What was the reaction of those who went out?

What did Jesus say to them?

6. Think of a place where missionaries go to serve. List five words that describe that location.

Do these words also describe your current place in life? Next to each word put a "T" for "True for my world" or "N" for "Not true for my world" to indicate whether these words apply or not.

THIS WEEK

Short-term missions trips are common experiences in youth groups, and often among the most significant experiences in people's lives. The Bible has a few stories in which people participated in a similar event. The Christian faith isn't something to be lived in secret, but something that propels us to care for others and be witnesses to what Christ has done. Through the story of the first short-term mission trip, this TalkSheet will allow your students to discuss missions and their role in it.

OPENER

Research the annual mission and service efforts your ministry supports and performs. Write them on a sheet of paper or whiteboard ahead of time, or add some fun and ask your students to see how many they know. Make sure to include overseas and local ministry efforts. What are the various purposes of the ministries? Are they all the same? Ask your students what they think the mission of your group is. What should we be doing in our community? In schools? In the world?

DISCUSSION

1. Have students share their answers. Ask if any of them have had to be a salesperson. What did they have to sell? How did that go? What's a missionary? See if they have a wide or narrow understanding of what a missionary is. Do missionaries have to serve overseas or serve full-time to be real missionaries? Can people be missionaries to their communities?

2. What definitions did they come up with? Do they center on the gospel? Do they include help and service in areas other than just spiritual? Ask your students where they learned about missions.

3. Matthew 28:18-20 is often called the Great Commission, one of Jesus' last commands to make disciples. How does the image of a "harvest field" help us understand more about ministry? Do other images (like a factory) work better?

4. Discuss what your students answered. Most students will focus on the "kingdom of God is near." Some might talk about the "Peace to this house," but that's seen as a greeting. Remind students that the kingdom focuses on the Messiah and reflects Jesus' message to others as he healed.

5. The people were excited about their service to God and what they did. Jesus reminded them that their confidence comes from their salvation, not their works (Matthew 7:22-23). He reminded them that salvation is possible because of God's all-powerful nature (Luke 10:22) and the work of his Son, Jesus. If you have time, discuss with your students how someone can do great works for God—even miraculous ones—and still not be a Christian.

6. Have students comment on their descriptions and how they fit in their lives. Do these things have to be present for a place to be a mission field? Can my neighborhood be a mission field? How are other mission fields different?

CLOSE

Tell students you have a question for them to consider: If it were clear God was calling them to reach out to another group, would they be willing to do that? What if it meant being a full-time missionary somewhere else? Ask students to close their eyes and reflect, pray, or just sit and think about their role in missions. After a minute, read Luke 10:2-3 and then pray for your students.

MORE

• **If your group has students who have been on mission trips, prearrange a panel discussion about missions with them. You'll want to give them the questions ahead of time, remind them to keep their answers short, and have a brief meeting ahead of time to coach them on what makes a good panel discussion (panels can be quite bad otherwise!). Focus on the work of the trip, not the effect in their lives. Other questions can focus on how the trip helped them understand missions and what their future involvement in missions and service will be.**

1. Write down as many occasions as you can remember when you were seriously in trouble with a parent, teacher, or coach.

WHO IS THE ACCUSER?

Jesus rescues the woman caught in adultery

(John 8:1-11)

Have you ever been accused wrongly by a parent or teacher and gotten into trouble anyway? How did you feel in that moment?

2. Do you think some sins are worse than others? Why or why not?

3. Read John 8:1-8. When Jesus said that those without sin could throw the first stone, what do you think he meant?

❑ No one is without sin, so no one should judge and punish others.
❑ Everyone is a sinner, so shouldn't we stone others too?
❑ Many of you in the crowd have also committed sexual sins.
❑ Haven't you heard what I have been teaching?
❑ God is establishing a new law that focuses on deliverance.

4. Read verses 9-11. Once the woman heard Jesus' response, what do you think she thought or felt?

5. Read Revelation 12:10. Who is our accuser and what does he do?

6. Read Matthew 7:1-5 and write three guidelines for how we should act toward others.

THIS WEEK

Some people have the mistaken perspective that God is out to get 'em. Rather than seeing God as one who offers us forgiveness through repentance, they see God as one who holds a grudge and gets really mad. The Bible shows that, while God is holy and cares about our faithfulness to him, he's also gracious and quick to forgive. So why do so many people still feel the weight of guilt and shame, with a little voice in their head reminding them about all their mistakes? This TalkSheet helps students see Christ's compassion and grace in action and understand that Satan is the accuser.

OPENER

Have students move to the right or left side of the room, or somewhere in between, that best reflects their opinions of the following questions.
Do most Christian high school students feel really good about their relationship with God (to the right) *or do they have a lot of shame and doubt* (left)? After students move, discuss why they chose where to stand. This can generate a lot of discussion, so ask your kids what factors people use to decide how their relationship with God is doing.

Then have students move based on these two questions:
Do most high school students carry a lot of guilt around about stuff they've done in the past (to their right) *or do they feel forgiven and free* (left)? Again, discuss the responses after students move.
When you attend church and/or youth group, do you feel better about your relationship with God (right) *or do you feel more ashamed* (left)? This is a tough one to discuss, but very worthwhile—especially if students are able to accurately reflect on this.

DISCUSSION

1. What's one of the earliest memories students have of getting in trouble at home? Did anyone get in trouble this past week? What's it like to be accused of doing something—even be punished—when innocent? Feel free to share an applicable and appropriate time in your own life as an example.

2. Students will have a range of answers from "all sin is sin" to a ranking system. Remind students that all sin goes against what God intends. Do your students think some acts, like murder, may involve more than one sin? What's the danger in thinking of some sins as little?

3. Ask students what would've happened to Jesus' message of forgiveness if the crowd were allowed to stone the woman. Remind students that if the woman was simply sent home, Jesus would've been seen as disobeying the law. Jesus effectively identified everyone in the crowd with the woman and her sin. They understood that at some point in their lives, they all deserved condemnation as well. Why is it important never to get so proud that we aren't aware of our own ability to disobey God?

4. Ask students about their answers. Do they think she changed her behavior after that encounter? Why or why not?

5. Why do people think God is an accuser? Should Christians feel like God is out to get them? Let students know that when we have thoughts of not being good enough for God to love, we need to pause and examine the source of those thoughts.

6. Have students report their answers and list them on the board. Do these verses say we can't take the speck out of someone else's eye? How do these verses say to do that?

CLOSE

It's not uncommon to feel like a gang has circled around you and each person is holding a rock to throw at you. The rocks may take forms other than a stone—they may look more like anger, criticisms, or harsh judgment. It's easy to put on God the thought that we'll never be good enough for him to love us. Of course, this story shows it's not about trying to earn God's forgiveness. Discuss with your students how they can receive God's forgiveness and how they can combat feelings that God is accusing them of not being good enough. Remind them that they, in turn, are not to accuse others, either.

MORE

• **The crowd had gathered in judgment of the woman who was caught in adultery. What are possible reasons that the man involved wasn't brought before Jesus too? Discuss with students whether we hold others to a higher standard than ourselves. Are we hard on our family members and intolerant of their behaviors, but expect a lot of understanding in return?**

• **Several other verses show Satan's role as the accuser. Students can check out these Bible passages: Job 1:6-10; Zechariah 3:1-2; John 10:10; and 1 Peter 5:8-9. Based on these verses, what is Satan's job? What's the focus of his accusations?**

1. **How do you usually express gratitude and thanks to others?**

❑ Card/note   ❑ Email or text message
❑ Smile   ❑ Give a gift
❑ A big hug   ❑ I'm not real good at it
❑ Telling them face-to-face
❑ Do something nice for them
❑ Other _____

THANKING CHRIST
The 10 lepers
(Luke 17:11-19)

2. **Read Luke 17:11-19. Come up with three possible reasons why the others didn't go back to thank Jesus.**

3. **Read 1 Thessalonians 5:16-18. Is it possible to be thankful in all situations? Why or why not?**

4. **Read Philippians 4:6-8. What effect can giving thanks have in giving us peace in our lives?**

Do we have a choice in deciding whether to be thankful or not?

5. **For each of the following, write down what you need to thank each of these people for, and the way to do it that would mean the most to that person.**

	I AM THANKFUL FOR:	I CAN LET THEM KNOW BEST BY:
Parent		
Friend		
Youth group leader(s)		
Jesus Christ		
Someone else		

THIS WEEK

We need to express our thankfulness to God. Many people today seem to feel they're owed certain blessings like health, respect, comforts, or fairness—and they get angry when others don't see that. It's part of our natural selfishness. What we often fail to realize is how much God has already done for us. This Talk-Sheet allows students to express their thankfulness as they learn about Jesus' healing of the 10 lepers.

OPENER

Get a video camera and head out to interview people around town who work in various jobs in which people have the opportunity to thank them. Ask these people how well people usually express gratitude to them. For starters, try a waitress or waiter, doctor, firefighter, pastor, janitor, hotel maid, and teacher. Follow up by asking them about the general gratitude of people they serve. Have someone edit this together into a fast-moving video of less than five minutes. Tell students you went out on the streets to talk to people about thankfulness.

DISCUSSION

1. Have your students share their answers here. Ask a few students to share a time when they did a great job of expressing gratitude. Did any students do a great job and *deserve* thanks, but didn't get it? Do students think most people they know are thankful? Are people more thankful in public or in private?

2. Students will have a variety of answers to this question. Is there a possible good reason or does Jesus' response eliminate that possibility? Ask students to help you craft a definition of ingratitude on the board.

3. Ask students in which situations it's most difficult to be thankful. For example, can they be thankful at school for getting an education? Can they be thankful even when circumstances aren't going their way? Working from your group's definition of ingratitude, help students see that thankfulness isn't dependent on everything going their way.

4. Ask students for their answers. Students might answer that it can be a reminder of what God has done and keep us focused on him and not on ourselves and our circumstances. Remind students that when we try to control our lives, worrying about the future and ourselves, we forget that God desires to be our peace as we trust him.

5. Just as the leper who went back to Jesus modeled for us, we need to pause and make sure to thank those who have provided for us in the past. Ask students what they noticed as they completed this question. Have they done a good job expressing thankfulness, or are there some ways they need to communicate their gratitude better?

CLOSE

Jesus met these lepers on the border between Samaria and Galilee (verse 11) as he traveled to Jerusalem. At a point between the three communities, Jesus met people in need and healed them (verse 14). One returned and was proclaimed well (verse 19) because of his faith. Tell students that their ability to be thankful to God even when they aren't getting their way can be a powerful demonstration of their faith and trust in Jesus.

MORE

• **Because of personality differences, different people may want to be thanked in different ways. These differences have been called love languages by Dr. Gary Chapman. For more information, visit www.fivelove-languages.com/learn.html. Have your students move into an area marked with one of these signs, and then have them discuss how these connect to giving thanks.**
• **One of the most fundamental problems with thankfulness is that we aren't thankful for who God created us to be. We don't like how we look or act, and we spend a lot of time wishing we were like someone else. Let students read Psalm 139:13-16 and discuss with them ways they can be thankful for who they are.**

Get in groups of four or so to complete this TalkSheet.

1. Some think there are five stages to grief. Match the word with the response that best illustrates it. Put Martha's and Mary's names next to the stage you think each woman was in.

Denial	I don't care and don't want to talk about it.
Anger	It's happened and I need to cope with it.
Bargaining	It's your/their fault that this happened to me because _____.
Depression	This didn't really happen.
Acceptance	If you do this, God, then I'll _____.

2. Read verse 21. When was the last time you felt like God didn't care?

___ Never   __ When I was a kid   ___ Over a year ago   ___ Last month   ___ This week

3. Read verses 33-36 and 38. Jesus knew he would raise Lazarus from the dead, so why do you think he cried?

4. Read verse 43. Why did Jesus mention Lazarus by name?

5. Is it significant that other people took off the grave clothes and not Jesus? Why or why not?

What things bind some of your friends like grave clothes—areas that keep them from allowing Jesus to give them life?

THIS WEEK

One of the most dramatic miracles in Jesus' entire ministry was the raising of Lazarus from the dead. It is a detailed story that shows Jesus' amazing compassion and his divine power over death. This TalkSheet teaches students about Jesus' nature as fully God and fully man through the scene of Jesus at the tomb of a close friend. It then shows how, through his compassion and power, he offers eternal life to us.

OPENER

This is a long story, but one worth reading before the students work on their TalkSheets. Lead off by reading verses 1-5 to set the scene. Have someone else read verses 17-27 and another read verses 32-37. Have another finish by reading verses 38-44. Have students then begin their TalkSheets.

Open the discussion time by talking about funerals. Some of your students may currently be in a period of grief, so be sensitive not to treat the topic lightly as you proceed. Have students describe some of the funerals they remember. What's the purpose of a funeral? How are some funerals different from others? Does going to a funeral strengthen or challenge your faith in God?

DISCUSSION

1. Go over the answers your students came up with for this question. You ought to have prepared a quick and appropriate story about grieving from your past that connects to one of these stages. What happens if a person doesn't grieve when they lose a friend or loved one? It's probable that your students have lost a close friend from school. This might be an opportunity to reflect on how people grieved at that time and what the situation is now.

2. Is it okay to experience times when we wonder where God is? What's our responsibility during those times? David had those times (Psalm 10). Why does David pray and remind himself of who God is (verses 16, 17) during those times?

3. When you think of Jesus crying at Lazarus' tomb, what images come to mind? Read Hebrews 4:15 and ask your students how Jesus' humanness gives them confidence in their prayers. Jesus' crying here was quiet tears (Acts 20:19) and not the loud wailing of the sisters (verse 33). Ask students why this might be.

4. What if Jesus had simply said, "Come forth"? Would *all* the dead in the tomb come out? Is there power in the words we say?

5. Ask students if ministry is up to God alone, up to us alone, or is it something men and women do with God? (If necessary, look at 2 Corinthians 5:11-21 and list what people do and what God does in ministry.) What are some of the "grave clothes" that bind people from experiencing Jesus' love? What did your students come up with as ways we can help others remove their "grave clothes"?

CLOSE

With sensitivity toward any students' current or past grieving, let students know it's when people pass away that we're reminded of how fragile and precious life is. The scene of Jesus standing before the tomb of Lazarus reminds us of his power over death, and also that he offers us eternal life. The unwrapping of the grave clothes reminds us of his desire for us to obey him and be holy as we do his work. His tears reveal his great compassion and love for people. In what ways do your students need to experience Christ's love this week? Wrap up by affirming to your students God's love for them.

MORE

• Mary and Martha are key characters in this story. An interesting extra might be to study the character of Martha. Have students check out the following verses: Luke 10:38-42; John 11:1, 20-24, 27, 39; and 12:2. What kind of person do you think Martha was? People can criticize Martha, but look at the verses and write down what Martha believed and how she was gifted. How does her personality compare to that of her sister, Mary? Which sister do you think you would most be like?

• This miracle shows Jesus' power, as God, over death. If Jesus claimed to be the Messiah who would come again and raise the dead, it was important for the Son of Man to show he could do that. For more, see John 5:25-29; 11:25-26; Revelation 21:4. How does Jesus' power over death give hope to people? How does it give hope when we think of our own eventual death?

1. **If I lose something, I usually (pick one):**

___ Don't worry about it. ___ Search for it till I find it.

___ Get mad. ___ Expect others to help.

___ Panic. ___ Get in trouble.

Have you ever believed you knew exactly where you were supposed to be, only to find that your directions were wrong and you were unusually lost? If so, describe that moment.

> # FINDING WHAT IS LOST
> ## The "lost" parables
> *(Luke 15:1-24)*

2. **What one item have you lost that you wish you had back?**

In 30 words or less, write a "lost and found" advertisement for your item, including why you want it back.

3. **Jesus tells three stories in Luke 15. Read verses 1 and 2. Who is Jesus talking to and what concerns do they have?**

Read the first story in Luke 15:3-7. Who does God rejoice over?

4. **Read Luke 15:11-24. For what purpose does the son want his inheritance?**

Once all his money is gone, how is the son lost? Is the son lost only after his money is gone?

What is the posture of the father as the son is returning home?

5. **Write "ME" in the box that fits you as it describes your relationship with God.**

I feel lost.	I need God's embrace.
I know where I am.	God and I are celebrating life together.

THIS WEEK

Besides stubbing a toe, one of life's most frustrating moments is when we lose something and can't find it. A different kind of frustration emerges when we get lost and can't find our way. Lostness is a common experience of all people, so when Jesus uses "lost" as a teaching lesson, the connection is clearly understood.

OPENER

To get things started, find unusual lost and found ads in your newspaper or at www.lostandfound.com and read them to your students. For more fun, bring in six items (the more unusual the better) from a local lost and found. Ask for volunteers to compete in a game called Lost and Found Stories. Give four students an item each and tell them to come up with a 60-second story about how the item was lost. Have the audience, by applause, identify the two that did the best with their stories, and have the other two storytellers sit down. Give these two the best of the six items for a final showdown. Have each tell a made-up story, get the audience's opinion and award the winner a prize. Have students describe what it feels like to discover they've lost something. Have any of them gotten separated from their parents on a trip when they were younger? How did their parents react to that?

DISCUSSION

1. Read off each one and have students raise their hands for the one they selected. Is there a right response? Why would someone get in trouble for losing something?
2. Did anyone write an ad they particularly liked? Have them read the ad. Have any of your students lost something and later found it in a lost and found? What did that feel like? How did they feel toward the person who found and returned it?
3. Ask students what the Pharisees complained about that caused Jesus to tell these stories. How did Jesus turn that around? What does Jesus show God is pleased with? Remind students that he's pleased when sinners repent—and he opposes the proud who don't need God (Proverbs 3:34 and 1 Peter 5:5).
4. For a son to ask for his portion at this point meant that he thought of his father as if he'd already died. What would your students' reactions have been if they were the dad? How do the father's actions in the story resemble God's? What's the father's reac-

tion even after the son has spent everything? What did the son realize when he was lost? How is the son's lostness similar to how some of your students' friends seem lost at times? What are ways we can get lost from where we need to be?

5. What's the difference between knowing where you are and *God* knowing where you are? Ask students to reflect on what *they* want from their relationship with God. What does *God* want? Remind students that when they feel lost, God is like the father in the story and waiting to welcome them at any point. Invite any students who may feel lost to set up a time to meet with an adult leader for follow-up conversations.

CLOSE

Each of these "lost" stories illustrates that God is able to forgive and is actively working to save all who respond—even those who choose to run away from him. This would be a great time to remind students of God's forgiveness. Jesus talks about repenting in these stories and illustrates it with the lost son's awareness of being lost once he realized he'd spent everything. Read Romans 6:23; Acts 3:19; and Romans 10:9-10. How is repentance similar to what the lost son says in Luke 15:18-19? How does asking God to forgive us of our sins help us be "found"? Challenge your students to examine their relationship with God, reminding them that you and others are available to talk to after the meeting.

MORE

• You can also start your meeting by showing selected scenes from the first episodes of the television show "Lost." Focus on scenes in which people realized they were lost. This could also work as part of your closing if you want to focus on Jesus' interpretation of these parables and connect with students about their own salvation.

• There are some good video adaptations of the prodigal son story on YouTube.com or GodTube.com. Check them out ahead of time. Start with: www.youtube.com/watch?v=Wl29ADCg8X4 or www.youtube.com/watch?v=e-00yOXmm_Y. After you show the video, ask students what they observed in the video. What does the video show that can be missed in just reading the story?

1. Imagine you just received $10,000 from a very distant relative who passed away. Write down in detail what you would do with that money.

WHAT IT REALLY MEANS TO BE RICH
The rich young man
(Matthew 19:16-24)

2. Which of the items that you own would be the most difficult for you to live without?

3. With a partner, look at Matthew 19:16-24. Why do you think riches make it so hard for people to follow Christ?

4. Imagine that the rich man had been reading the Old Testament and ran across the following verses. With your partner, look up the following verses and write down what he might conclude for each pair.

    1 Chronicles 4:10 and Jeremiah 29:11—

    Proverbs 30:8-9 and Jeremiah 9:23-24—

5. Proverbs 23:4 says, "Do not wear yourself out to get rich." Give two or three examples of how people wear themselves out to get rich.

6. Draw a stick figure person on the line that best describes your feelings.

◄ • ►

I'm content
with what I have.

I often think about
what I want to buy.

I am very
discontented.

THIS WEEK

Teens and adults are bombarded with advertising, calling on them to acquire the latest trend in fashions, the newest gadgets, or the "in" experiences. This TalkSheet gives your teens a chance to explore the topic of wealth and reflect on the materialistic forces present in their culture. We need to realize we have immense wealth, comparatively speaking, and need to learn to be generous and reflect Christ's values for the poor and oppressed.

OPENER

To start the discussion, get your students discussing whether they think they're conditioned to recognize and purchase certain brands. Start by showing very short video segments of popular commercials. Play just a small segment and see if your teens instantly recognize them. Or start a common advertising slogan and see if your students can finish it. Get these from TV, the Internet, or the newspaper. Divide the room into two teams and see which team answers first. On the board, write the names of two competing brands and see which is preferred by your students and why. Do this for four to five pairs of major brands (soda, clothing, cars, peanut butter, etc.). Why do many people have strong preferences for particular brands? Does advertising really have an influence? Why or why not?

DISCUSSION

1. Ask some of your students to share what they wrote. Was it easy for your students to do this or difficult? What if it was $1,000? Would that have been easier? $100,000? Did anyone spend it on one item? Did anyone give part of it away?

2. Ask for some of the items your students wrote down here. Keep track on the board, if you want, to show which were the most popular. This could be a difficult exercise for some students. Ask students why it would be difficult to live without that particular item.

3. Write what Paul wrote to Timothy in 1 Timothy 6:9: "Those who want to get rich fall into temptation and a trap and into many foolish and harmful desires that plunge people into ruin and destruction." Ask students to help you rewrite that so its meaning is clearer for high school students. What desires does getting rich promote? Do your students feel happier when they get something new (like new clothes)?

4. If a person only read the first two verses, what would he or she think about what God desires? What if someone only read the other two verses? How do these four verses balance each other? What's our responsibility to the poor? Push your students here as most students will think they're not rich enough to help those in need.

5. Is there a line of income or wealth where "normal" ends and "rich" begins? What things do people do to try to get rich? Do people work hard at *getting* rich or *looking* like they're rich? What's the goal of life?

6. Write on the board, show on an overhead, or pass out slips of paper with Philippians 4:11-13 on it. What principles does Paul put into practice as they relate to his circumstances? What would change if we applied those principles to our lives?

CLOSE

What's our responsibility with the stuff we possess? What does it mean to be a steward of what God has given us? Who is the owner? We can easily lose our way and think that fulfillment comes through gathering wealth and possessions. This line is different for each of your students. It's the attitude and proper perspective on what God has given us.

MORE

• If you have an Internet connection for all to see, take students to www.globalrichlist.com and type in $4,000—about what a high school senior could make in a year. Show students where that annual income ranks in the world. Then type in $40,000—what a teacher in a local school might make—and show them where that is on the world's wealth list. Ask students whether this makes them rich or not. What does "rich" look like?

• Find a good photographer and ask him or her to go around the community with you and capture pictures that show the level of poverty in your own community—an existence that many may not be aware of. Be sensitive to people as you do this, and be aware that many students in your group may come from families at or below the poverty line. But most students are unaware of the issues people in their own communities face, and you can show that though a powerful digital slide show. Close by asking your students, "So what do we do about this?"

• There are lots of great resources along these lines. Youth Specialties' One Life Revolution (www.oneliferevolution.org) and a terrific book entitled *Generation Change* by Zach Hunter will help challenge your students to make a financial difference. Compassion International also offers opportunities for your group to sponsor a child somewhere in the world.

1. Give a definition of what it means to be fair.

NO FAIR!
The workers in the vineyard
(Matthew 20:1-16)

2. Read Matthew 20:1-16. Would you have reacted any differently?

3. Read Matthew 19:27. Which of the following best represents Peter's concern?

___ I've left everything for your kingdom. I hope to get something in return.

___ How can you give rewards to others when I've been following you for years?

___ You said you'd build your church on me. Who are these other people?

___ Peter has the wrong motives for serving Jesus.

4. Sarah spent most of her life uninterested in the things of God, avoiding church. In fact, not only was she involved in all sorts of wild stuff, she was downright mean to the kids who called themselves Christians. This continued well past high school until she was about 25 years old, when she had a bad drug overdose at a party and ended up in a coma. As she breathed her last, she confessed her sin and asked God to forgive her and accept her as his child—which he did. And he threw a big party for her in heaven.

Should God have forgiven Sarah?

How do you feel about the "throwing a party" part?

Do you think some people would resent the fact that she was able to be mean her whole life and then receive such a welcome?

5. Which of the following best describes what's meant by "the last will be first and the first will be last"?

a. Those who let others go first are better than those at the front of the line.

b. In the end, the line will be reversed and the people at the end will be first.

c. There is no "first" or "last" in God's kingdom—all are equally his children.

d. We need to be aware of times when we're kind solely to earn God's approval.

THIS WEEK

A common cry on a playground or at any sporting event is, "That's not fair!" It's not just in sports—we can feel slighted when others seem to get more recognition, attention, or benefits than we do while we're overlooked. In God's economy, grace is given freely to those who respond to the gospel. It's not something we can work toward. This story shows we're never too far from God to receive forgiveness, and that God's love is given equally to all.

OPENER

Do your students think other people get more breaks than they do? Write the phrase "That's Not Fair!" on the board. Hand out blank cards to your students and have them write down instances when something unfair happened to them. On the left side of the board, write down some prompts such as brothers and sisters, teachers, coaches, classes, work, other families, and church. Have students hand them back in and read through them, making sure not to mention specific names. Another person can write some of the key phrases on the board. What do you notice about the items your group mentioned? Does anyone really feel like life has been fair? Is life supposed to be fair? Is God fair?

DISCUSSION

1. Have your students share their definitions. Write some of the key phrases on the board. Do your students equate fairness with goodness? Can someone be fair and not good? How about good and not fair? Don't go too fast on these two concepts—let students think about people they know.

2. What main objection did the workers have? Were they right to feel that way? What did students say about how they would've reacted? Don't we say "that's not fair" for things a lot less important than this story?

3. What did your students write down as the best explanation? In what ways is Peter saying, "That's not fair"? Peter wants to know what the rewards are for being a disciple of Jesus and whether he'll get a greater reward since he's been following Jesus longer and with greater commitment than others. Can your students think of verses that discuss what God's rewards are? Which of Peter's responses are based on human effort alone? Is it easy to feel like you're working hard so God will like you more?

4. Remind students that all can experience God's sal-vation equally and that not a moment arrives when some get more of God's favor than others. This story confronts some of the common ways that we think about being a Christian—the idea that we have to work to earn our good standing with God. Have two students read Ephesians 2:8-10 (a great reminder of how people are redeemed and what the purpose of their work is) and Matthew 19:17 (a reminder that God is good and generous). Ask students what those verses say about God's opinion of us.

5. Ask students if they think there's favoritism in the church. Is there favoritism in God's kingdom? Let students know that God's grace is unmerited favor—we can't do anything to deserve it. What did your students answer for this question? Which ones focus on what we do? Which focus on what God has done? Where have you and your students been in the trap of expecting to get something in return for good work, service, or obedience?

CLOSE

Ask students to think about the ways in which God has been generous to them. List them on the board. Help students think about the physical, social, cultural, spiritual, material, and mental aspects of life. When done with that list, ask if they think they should have more than this. Remind students that the greatest gift of God was his Son, Jesus, and the presence of the Holy Spirit in their lives.

MORE

• **A contemporary example of people arguing fairness is arguing with referees at sporting events. Why do people argue with referees? What's the purpose? For some examples of bad referee calls, see jettingthroughlife. blogspot.com/2006/07/top-10-worst-referee-calls. html. A classic online video is www.fliggo.com/video/ xKaGWwIL.**

• **Deuteronomy 24:14-15 provided guidelines for how and when a person should be paid for such work. A biblical example of a person not feeling treated fairly can be found at the end of Luke 15 when the older brother was angry at his father for celebrating the return of his younger brother. The younger brother had left the family, spent his inheritance, and returned full of regret for his actions. The father threw a big feast to celebrate his return, and the elder son thought it wasn't fair. Can your students relate to the older son?**

1. Give a definition of *greatness*.

2. Mark the following as VG (very great), G (great), and NG (not very great):

____ babysitting your younger siblings without getting paid

____ finishing first in a marathon

____ having dinner with the President of the United States

____ getting better grades than your friends

____ helping out at the homeless shelter

____ being nominated for the scholarship your best friend was hoping to get

____ having a maid at home to clean up after you

____ making it to the national championship with your sports team

____ doing the dishes after supper

____ cleaning the bathroom

BEING GREAT, PART 1

James and John

(Mark 10:35-45)

3. Read Mark 10:35-45. What do James and John want? Why do they think they deserve this?

What did Jesus say would be required for that to happen?

How did the other disciples respond?

4. Take a look at Philippians 2:5-11. List the steps down that Jesus took to come to earth on the left side, and the resulting steps up to the greatness given to him on the right side.

_____   _____

_____   _____

_____   _____

Jesus died on the cross and rose from the dead

5. What are two ways people at your school try to be great?

Looking at question #4, what does Jesus show us about how we're to be great?

THIS WEEK

Greatness and prestige are highly esteemed in our society. As they try to achieve greatness, most people worry about how they can get ahead, how they can outdo their neighbors, how they can build their resumes, and so on. Jesus had an entirely different approach to greatness. The challenge this week is to lead students to understand greatness by discussing the model of servanthood left by Christ for us to follow.

OPENER

Begin your discussion time by asking students to get into groups of three and make a list of the top five greatest people that have ever lived. Allow some time for each group to share their lists and ask them to explain why they chose each person. What qualities did (or does) that person have that made (or makes) him or her great?

DISCUSSION

1. What would your students like to be great at doing? How do your kids define greatness? Do they have a desire to be great? What does it mean to be great in their school? Who determines greatness? Students may vary in what they think qualifies as greatness. At this point in the lesson, don't give your definition of greatness.

2. How did your students rate the list of activities? What seemed to be the greatest achievement? What was deemed least great? Engage in conversation about how they decided which of these were great or not.

3. Share how greatness is acquired through servanthood. Though Jesus is the Son of the High King, he made himself like a servant. His purpose for coming to earth was not to be served, but to serve. Is greatness doing something well, being respected by others, or having others think you do something great?

4. Jesus took on the attitude of a servant, making himself nothing in his society. Discuss with your students Jesus' divine nature versus the nature he took on as a servant. Notice the magnitude of Jesus' greatness in verses 9-11. Can your students give other examples of how Jesus served others?

5. Ask students where greatness comes from. What's the source of greatness? Is it something we just do, something we work to develop, or something we're given? If people see us instead of Christ in us, is that greatness? Knowing what Jesus values, what steps are your students willing to take toward true greatness and away from how the world may define greatness?

CLOSE

James and John wanted to know how to be great. As Jesus' disciples, they had the opportunity to observe his character on many occasions. Over and over again, Jesus taught and modeled servanthood to his disciples. Discuss with your students how they can be great through serving others.

MORE

• **Starting off with the card game President/Scum of the Earth is another option. Rules can be found at www.pagat.com/invented/scum_of_the_earth.html. After playing the game, students can talk about how it feels to be "scum" and how the president treated the scum. Students that reach the status of President and Vice President can also reflect on the way they worked to get to the top (i.e., by treating others like scum).**

• **Check out how loving God and others ties in with servanthood: Galatians 5:13-15; Matthew 22:34-40; John 13:1-17. Break students up into groups and assign each group a passage. After 10 minutes, give students the opportunity to share their observations about love and servanthood with the group, and how these observations can translate into living love and service to others.**

(Thanks to Holly Birkey for the TalkSheet idea)

1. Which of the following skills is something you do well? Put an "X" next to your top three.

____ Cooking	____ Basketball/volleyball
____ Singing	____ Gardening
____ Drawing	____ Band/choir
____ Reading	____ Text messaging
____ Sleeping	____ Running/swimming
____ Dancing	____ Listening
____ Baseball/soccer	____ Writing
____ Working	____ Praying
____ Cars/bikes	____ Studying
____ Video	____ Other

2. List three to five talents, interests, responsibilities, or skills you know you have or that someone has pointed out to you. Put a check mark next to the ones that define you best— in that when you're doing them, you feel wide awake and in the zone.

3. Write a quick definition for what it means to be faithful in what we do. Give any real-life examples of when you've been faithful.

4. Read Matthew 25:14-30. The last servant didn't respect the master's talents. God is the creator and giver of the skills and talents you possess. Put an "X" on the line below that best depicts how the two of you would judge your use of his gifts to you:

◄••►

| Haven't thought much about it | Struggling to be consistent | Working on being faithful | Being faithful with regularity |

5. Draw a circle around the choices above (in questions #1 and #2) that would be very difficult for you to give up. Now read verses 21 and 29 and write a sentence below that summarizes the results of being faithful with your skills and talents.

For this coming week, list two faithful ways you can let God use your talents and skills:

THIS WEEK

This parable focuses on being faithful with our talents and gifts in light of the coming return of Christ. Students will explore this teaching of Jesus and plan for faithful actions in their own lives. It's important to make sure this lesson doesn't emphasize salvation by works. The parable before this one in Matthew is about being prepared inwardly, so the two need to be balanced.

OPENER

Using a melodrama format, read Matthew 25:14-30 while four students act out up front what you read. It would be best to pick students prior to the meeting and practice it to help it be funny and also clear. You ought to strongly consider picking students who will hold students' attention and give the melodrama some sizzle. It's also important not to use the same students who usually get chosen—to consciously work for diversity in who gets up front.

After the melodrama skit, say, "One of the key words you see in this story is *faithful*. What are some other words or phrases that may help us better understand what this means?" List these on a whiteboard or newsprint up front. Make sure the word *responsibilities* gets on the board.

DISCUSSION

1. Students will check a variety of items. Pick four or five of the choices (it's fun to pick "text messaging" as one of them) and ask, "How many of you put a mark beside _____?" Ask students how they decided they were good at their choices.

2. Students who deal with poor self-esteem may have problems making this list. Be sensitive and offer examples. As students write their answers, reread verse 21. Tell students that some of the items on their lists might be considered small, but are still valuable and important to list.

3. Have students share their definitions. Get as many as you can, then have students who wrote examples to share them. Point out words from the board that are part of various responses. It would be good for you or other adults in the room to have a few quick examples from your own lives ready to share in case this discussion slows down.

4. Ask students if it's possible to rank the three servants. The first two were equally faithful, using their talents to double what the master had given them. What was the chief problem with what the last servant did?

5. Sometimes what we do defines who we are in school. We get labeled as an athlete, or a band member, or a person who likes to study—and each of us is much more than that. Look at your responses for the last two questions and consider what God desires from your life.

CLOSE

Pass out small slips of paper or index cards to the students. Have them write on the card their answers to question #2. They can add any other talents, interests, responsibilities, or skills they've thought of since then. Tell them they're going to offer these back to God. Have an area up front, maybe with a cross or picture, that symbolizes Christ and has the feel of an altar. Play meditative music in the background and ask students to prayerfully consider offering their talents, interests, responsibilities, or skills back to God and let him lead them as they serve God.

MORE

• **The parable of the talents is focused on our outside lives—being faithful in our work or service for God. In contrast, the parable before this one in Matthew—the 10 bridesmaids—focused on being faithful in our inside, spiritual lives. Which is easier for your students— to think of the Christian life as something we *do* or something we *are*?**

• **This lesson has the potential to make some students feel inferior, particularly because certain skills and or talents are seen as superior to others. You will want to make sure not to let this happen.**

THE MESSIAH COMES TO JERUSALEM
The triumphal entry of Jesus
(Matthew 21:1-11)

1. Have you ever made a triumphant entry that changed the outcome of something (for example, during a discussion, game, play, musical number, or work)? Describe the scene and how your impact changed the situation.

2. Jesus entered Jerusalem on a donkey to fulfill prophecy from the Old Testament. Read Zechariah 9:9 and list the ways Jesus fulfilled this particular prophecy.

3. Read Luke's version in Luke 19:28-44. In verses 41-44 Jesus weeps over Jerusalem and her people. Why does he do that?

4. The people on the road that day were mostly from Galilee, meaning they'd seen Jesus do miracles and knew who he was. The people in Jerusalem had maybe only heard about him. Describe the possible different reactions to Jesus by those who knew him versus those who had only heard about him.

5. Jesus went to Jerusalem for a specific purpose. Flip back one chapter and read Matthew 20:17-19. Jesus knew what would happen if he went, so why did he go? What do you think would've happened if he hadn't gone to Jerusalem?

THIS WEEK

At the end of Jesus' public ministry he arrived like a king at Jerusalem. This arrival began a series of God-orchestrated events leading to the death and resurrection of Jesus. This TalkSheet gives students an opportunity to understand the significance of Jesus' arrival as well as how it can impact their lives today.

OPENER

Start by asking your students to think through the movies they've watched and describe the moments when a hero triumphantly arrives on the scene (e.g., The evil emperor Commodus arriving to take the throne in *Gladiator*, Spiderman arriving to save Mary Jane in *Spider Man 3*, and so on). As students give their own examples, write them down on a whiteboard or newsprint up front. Get a good list and ask students why those scenes are so easy to remember. How do these entrances impact the story? Do they build excitement and anticipation for those who are watching? Give students a few minutes to respond to each question. Follow up answers if you feel more could be gained from their responses.

Tell students you're going to read about a triumphant entry in the Bible. As in most movies, this arrival marked a serious change in the storyline, one that ultimately affected the ending of the story. Ask for a volunteer student with a good voice to stand up and read Matthew 21:1-11.

DISCUSSION

1. Students will likely answer this question very differently. Spend some time encouraging students that each of them has made a large impact and contribution in some situation. Though we may often be the last to know of our own impact, it still happens. Take a few minutes and let some students share how they've impacted things in their life.
2. Remind students that the fact that Jesus fulfilled Old Testament prophecies is important. Have students consider the ways Jesus fulfilled the Zechariah passage: the people rejoiced and shouted in triumph, Jesus came to Jerusalem as the king, he never sinned, he's victorious over life and death, he was humble when he told people not to tell of his great miracles, and he arrived at Jerusalem on a donkey's colt. If time allows, talk about the importance of the Old Testament prophecies being fulfilled.

3. Have a student reread verses 41-44 to the group. Ask for their responses regarding why Jesus wept over the people of Jerusalem.
4. This is a key lesson of the passage. Take some time to discuss the difference between knowing Jesus personally and only hearing about him. Can you know somebody if you don't spend time with the person? Challenge your students not only to hear about Jesus at church, but also to spend time with him throughout the week by reading their Bibles.
5. The first part of the question is fairly straightforward. Make a list up front of reasons why Jesus continued on to Jerusalem. Be certain to include to be betrayed, beaten, crucified, and rise again. The second question will get many different answers. Guide the discussion so that students can understand why the death and resurrection of Jesus is so important and necessary to the gospel message.

CLOSE

Jesus' arrival in Jerusalem started a chain of God-orchestrated events that has changed the world. He arrived as a king to those who knew him, and left as Lord and Savior of the entire earth. Give your students a few moments to reflect on their own relationship with Jesus and how well they know him. Lead them in a time of prayer, thanking Jesus for triumphantly arriving on the scene, and asking him to play a larger role in our own lives.

More

• **This lesson could easily be turned into a full-out gospel presentation. As you discuss the differences between knowing Jesus and knowing *of* him. Challenge the students: Do they really know Jesus personally, or have they only heard about him? Verses to take them through could include John 1:12; 5:24; Romans 3:23; 6:23; 5:8; and Titus 3:5. Give students a chance to respond. This is a great illustration to use to challenge students who have attended church their entire lives, but have never accepted Jesus as Lord.**

• **At the end of the lesson give each student an index card and a pen. Have them write the names of friends and family who might have heard about Jesus but don't know him personally. Challenge them to take that card with them and pray for those people every day. Encourage them to share what they've learned here with the people on their list. It could open a door to lead that person to Christ.**

(Thanks to Tom Carpenter for the TalkSheet idea)

1. Finish this sentence: When my mom or dad asks me to help around the house, I _____

_____.

What's the messiest job or chore that you've ever done?

What has been the most difficult job or chore you've ever done?

What job around the house do you hate most?

THIS JOB STINKS!
Jesus models how to serve
(John 13:1-17)

2. Read John 13:1-5. What does verse 3 mean?

How does that allow Jesus the ability to easily do what he does in the next verse?

3. Read verses 6-10. Which of the following best explains Peter's reaction?

Peter didn't understand what Jesus was doing and was telling a joke.

Peter was embarrassed that Jesus had to do this servant's act.

He wanted to have Jesus' complete healing, not just the ceremonial one of only his feet.

He didn't want Jesus to wash his feet, so he tried to get Jesus to quit.

He needed a bath anyway, so he was making light of that fact.

4. Read what Jesus said in verses 13-17. Rewrite this into a single sentence:

5. If you were a teacher and had to grade yourself on your willingness to serve others, what grade would you get? Explain the reasons for your grade.

Write down the name of one person you believe God wants you to serve this week and what you could do to serve him or her in a meaningful way:

THIS WEEK

One of the most powerful moments of Jesus' intentional modeling for his disciples (and for us!) was when he performed one of the most menial services of that time—the simple act of washing others' feet. In a moment when the disciples were unwilling to serve others, the great Teacher willingly performed the courtesy and then instructed his disciples to do the same. The challenge remains that we're to serve in ways that confront our pride.

OPENER

Before your opening, find 12 dirty jobs—visit the Web site of the TV show *Dirty Jobs* for some ideas—and choose six either/or pairs to make the decision difficult as to which job a high schooler would prefer. Find 10 to 12 pictures of various human feet and create a computer slideshow presentation. Run it continuously behind you for the opening (or the whole lesson!). Are there chores, jobs, or duties you don't enjoy doing? Tell students you're going to play Would You Rather and ask them to stand. Announce one pair of jobs at a time and have students choose which one they'd rather do by moving to one side of the room or the other. Get a few quick reactions from students as to why they made their choice. Repeat this for each pair and then have students sit down.

DISCUSSION

1. Quickly have students announce their answer to the first sentence completion. Keep it moving fast and lively and try to get most of the students—if not all—to answer it. It's a safe one. For the following questions, highlight the messiest and feel free to follow it up. Do your students enjoy messy and difficult jobs or do they shy away from them?
2. Washing guests' feet was a common courtesy of the day. Everyone wore sandals or no shoes at all, and the washing of feet when a guest entered a home was a hospitable way to clean off the dirt, sand, and sweat so that the eating area could be kept clean. Why did the disciples choose not to wash the others' feet? Jesus is stating aloud who he is, and it is from this strength that he's able to serve in a menial capacity. Our insecurity and concern over what others think about us comes from sinful pride that keeps us from being able to give ourselves away for the sake of others.

3. Have students discuss their answers. How does Peter's personality play a role in how he acted? What do you think the other disciples did? Do you think the disciples understood what Jesus was saying?
4. Ask for students to share their sentences. What's the significance of these verses? How does your church do at fulfilling these? What would change if we intentionally put this into practice on a regular basis?
5. Gently point out to students that we're often like the disciples, unwilling to serve. Sinful pride, selfishness, and concern about what others think of us prevent us from reflecting Christ. Mention some verses that remind students of their identity in Christ and reinforce their faith and trust in him, enabling them to serve others. Challenge students to allow the Holy Spirit to take the lead in how they can show Jesus' love for others this week—specifically, by humbling themselves to serve someone difficult.

CLOSE

Before the lesson, write this goal of the spiritual formation process on small slips of paper, enough for all your students: "Conforming to the image of Christ for the sake of others." It's from Robert Mulholland's book *Invitation to a Journey*. Then write the phrase on the board before students arrive for the lesson. Encourage them to reflect this week on this saying and to be alert for ways they're reflecting the character of Jesus in how they act toward others.

MORE

• **If you've never performed a footwashing service, this would be a great time to do so with your students. Divide them up by gender, boys on one side and girls on the other, so boys are washing boys' feet and girls are washing girls' feet. Play a series of worshipful songs in the background and provide a small basin of water and towel for each pair of students. All students will "wash" the feet of those sitting next to them. Check online for helpful Web sites—this is an important and regular service in some denominations. Start with en.wikipedia.org/wiki/Feet_washing and www.kencollins.com/how-06.htm for a fuller understanding of the service and details about how to conduct it.**

1. Which of the following have the strongest connection? Check up to three.

❑ Electric fan and power plant

❑ Glue and pieces of paper

❑ Tree and soil

❑ Two people on cell phones

❑ Two Yankees baseball fans

❑ Two close friends

❑ Mother and her child

❑ Person's arm and shoulder

❑ Branch and its vine

❑ St. Louis and New Orleans

THE TRUE VINE
Being connected to Jesus
(John 15:1-11)

2. What's your favorite fruit to eat?

How did you learn to like that fruit?

3. Read John 15:1-6. How does a branch bear fruit?

How does Jesus say you can bear fruit?

What is the fruit?

4. Read the following verses and write next to each one how Jesus says we're to remain in him:

John 6:56—

John 8:31—

John 15:9-10—

5. Take a look at the fruitful qualities from Galatians 5:22-23 listed below. For each, ask yourself, "Have I been more _____ than I was a year ago?" Record an "M" if you've seen more of that fruit, "S" if you've seen about the same level of that quality, or "L" if it's been less obvious since a year ago.

LOVE _____   JOY _____   PEACE _____

PATIENCE _____   KINDNESS _____   GOODNESS _____

SELF-CONTROL _____   FAITHFULNESS _____   GENTLENESS _____

THIS WEEK

It's not uncommon to hear students talk about their personal relationships with Jesus. This can mean different things to different people, so this lesson helps define how Jesus viewed its meaning. Not only does Jesus provide a great visual example for the disciples, but he also reminds them of a function of the relationship—to be fruitful and live a godly life.

OPENER

Divide the students into equal groups of no more than eight each. Tell them they're going to make a short commercial for a fruit. The purpose of the commercial is to explain why that fruit is the best fruit. Use apples, bananas, grapes, oranges, raspberries—and give one group tomatoes just for fun. Give students a few minutes to prepare their commercials, then perform them. Compliment each group and then ask students which commercial they found most convincing. Why? Did the tomato group convince anyone that a tomato is really a fruit? Can your students tell you what's involved in the fruit-growing process? Jesus uses fruit as an illustration of what it means to be a Christian.

DISCUSSION

1. Ask students to share what they selected and why. You may have to explain how some pairs are connected (St. Louis and New Orleans share a major river…and jazz). Pay attention to the criteria students used (or didn't use) to make their selections. What choices didn't get any marks?

2. Let students share their favorite fruits. Keep track of the most popular choices. Did they love fruit from the beginning or did they *learn* to like fruit? Ask students to name the most unusual fruit they've ever eaten.

3. Remind students that a branch can only bear fruit if it remains connected to the vine. The power and growth of the branch comes not from itself, but from the vine. Discuss students' answers with them—the idea that fruit can mean other people coming to faith in Christ (Romans 1:13), our own growth in obeying God (Romans 6:22), and the fruit of the Holy Spirit (Galatians 5:22-23).

4. Let students share their answers for what they found. Tell them that to remain is not a one-time event, but a continual connectedness in which Christ is the source and power in our lives. To remain means we first must accept Jesus as our Savior and then keep holding on to him through obedience and knowing his Word. What's the connection, the bond, between Jesus and his followers? You can read Romans 8:38-39 and 1 Corinthians 6:19-20 for perspective on this question.

5. List the fruits of the Spirit (Galatians 5:22-23) on the board. Ask students to think about these fruits in their lives. Are they more loving than they were a year ago? More joyful? More peaceful? And so on. Give them a few minutes to write down how each of these fruits are growing in their lives. Close by reminding them there's a relationship with God that serves as the source for what we do in our lives. While Jesus, as the Vine, offers that relationship, we have a responsibility to remain connected to him.

CLOSE

Read 1 Corinthians 3:9, "For we are God's co-workers; you are God's field, God's building." Review with students their job as the branches. What is Jesus' role as the Vine? If they're involved in a ministry, is it something that "God does through us" (Acts 15:4)? How do the fruits of the Spirit show others what God is doing in our lives?

MORE

• As a visual extra, have bowls of fruit sitting around the room as students show up. Those listening to Jesus understood what the imagery of the vine meant to Israel, God's people (Isaiah 5:7; Jeremiah 6:9; Hosea 10:1). Jesus uses that image to claim his role as the Messiah, God in flesh, the true vine. Consequently, he has the power and position to be the center and source of the work in the kingdom of God.

1. Who regularly prays for you? Write down their names below.

Besides yourself, whom have you prayed for in the last month, and what was it about?

2. Read John 17:1-5. Looking at verse 5, what's Jesus praying about?

3. Jesus prays for his disciples in verses 11-19. Give an example of what each of the following means:

They are in the world, but not of the world—

They may have the full measure of joy within them—

They are sanctified by God's truth—

4. Jesus prays for *you* in his prayer. What does Jesus pray for in verses 20-26? Check all that apply.

a. That you will have unity and harmony with other Christians.
b. That your harmony with others would be in unity with Christ and God's purposes.
c. That others will know God's love because of your love for others.
d. That you will someday see Jesus in his glory in heaven.

5. Why do you think unity was such a big part of Jesus' last prayer for his disciples and for the church today?

THIS WEEK

At the end of Jesus' life on earth, John records a prayer in which Jesus prays for all his followers. It's often called a high priestly prayer because Jesus is praying in a way that resembles a priest's role as mediator between people and God. The unique thing is that Jesus prays for *us* in this prayer, the themes of which provide the focus of this TalkSheet discussion.

OPENER

During the week before this lesson, find some written prayers and references to prayer from magazines, newspapers, and online. Print a collection that shows a range of approaches and different thinking about prayer. Have students get in groups with others around them and pass these papers out so each group has at least two prayers to read. Give your students a few minutes to read through the prayers. Then ask: To whom is the prayer written? What's the focus of the prayer? Why write a prayer? What do your students think about written prayers—are they authentic when read, or is it better to pray spontaneously whatever comes to your heart?

DISCUSSION

1. Have some students share what they wrote about who prays for whom. How do they know who's praying for them? Do they think about that regularly? Does it matter if we're prayed for regularly, or not prayed for? For whom are your students regularly praying? Why did they choose those people to pray for? Why pray at all?

2. It's important to remember that Jesus, as God, has always existed and that he wasn't created when he came to earth as a baby. Read Colossians 1:15-17. What does "He is before all things" mean? Read Philippians 2:6-8; what does "being in very nature God" say about who Jesus was before Creation?

3. Jesus says that the world hated him and that they'll hate his followers too. Ask your students if they've seen that in their lives. How can someone be full of joy when the world is against them? *Sanctify* means to set apart, consecrate, or dedicate. How does God's Word help us to be dedicated? How do your students react to the idea of being set apart to be a Christian?

4. All of these are present in Jesus' prayer. Unity is a goal that exists because of what Christ has done to extend forgiveness to us and isn't meant to draw attention to ourselves or our churches. The goal of our love is for people to understand who God is (Matthew 5:16). How has your group's unity fared during the last month? What can your students do to promote unity and love among those in your group? What's significant about the fact that Jesus prayed for each one of us?

5. Often people's biggest objections to church are that it's boring and that the people there aren't very nice. The biggest temptation for people within churches is to focus on the wrong things. What does Jesus' prayer tell us about what we should focus on?

CLOSE

Tell the students you're going to work on a group prayer together—the ultimate prayer. What should it include? Write ideas from your students on the board. What are the things we should be praying for in a prayer that will last a long time? After you have done this for four to five minutes, arrange students' ideas in a format that resembles (1) praying about who God is, (2) praying about who God wants us be, and (3) praying for God's help in being who he wants us to be. Have someone type the prayer and distribute it at the next meeting or through email.

MORE

• **The words *glory* and *glorify* are prominent in this prayer. For further study, students can note each time these words are used in the chapter and what their usage means. Have students look up Exodus 29:42-43; 33:18-23; John 1:14; 12:23; and 2 Peter 1:16-18. Then have them read John 14:23-24 and 17:24-26. What do these verses tell us about God's glory? What difference does it make for Christians to be aware of God's glory being present in their lives?**

• **Spend some time talking about prayer with your students. Encourage your students to invest in their prayer lives. For one week, have them journal each night about their prayers that day, keeping track of what they pray about and when. Ask students what they expect to discover. What percentage of their prayers is about what they want? What would happen if students wrote out their prayers before praying them? You may want to establish a Web page where students and others can post four-sentence prayers on a discussion board. This can promote a unity of and focus on prayer among your students during the week.**

1. When your church, or a group at your church, eats a meal together, what do they do besides eat?

What are some of the foods you can always count on seeing there?

THE LAST SUPPER
Jesus prepares the disciples for his death
(Matthew 26:17-30)

2. When your family wants to celebrate over a meal, what do they do?

Order carry-out   Eat pizza   Go to a nice restaurant

Watch a movie and eat snacks   Prepare a big meal at home   Invite friends over

3. Read Matthew 26:17-18 and Mark 12:12-15. What kind of preparations did Jesus make for the last meal with his disciples?

Read Exodus 12:3, 6, 14-17. What did some of the disciples have to do?

4. Read Matthew 26:20-25. Why did the disciples ask Jesus if it would be one of them who would betray him?

___ They knew they had doubts.   ___ They were being polite.

___ They didn't want to disappoint the Master.   ___ They were scared of the Romans.

___ They believed, but were really distressed.   ___ They were questioning themselves.

Do you think the disciples were surprised to find out that Judas would be the one to betray Jesus?

5. Read Matthew 26:26-27. What does the bread represent?

Read verses 27-28—What does the wine represent and what does that provide?

Read verse 29—What is Jesus talking about here?

Read verse 30—If you were there and chose to sing one meaningful song or hymn at the last supper with Jesus, what would you choose and why?

THIS WEEK

As Jesus neared the time of his death and resurrection, he gathered his disciples together for an intimate Passover celebration. Through the symbols of the bread and the cup, Jesus instructed them to remember him and his atoning sacrifice. These symbols and the meal, known as the Lord's Supper, Communion, or the Eucharist, have become one of the most important sacraments of the church, a reminder of the central belief of Christianity. This TalkSheet gives ample opportunity to discuss various aspects of this key church practice with your students.

OPENER

Do your students remember the first time they watched others taking communion? Did they understand what it was about at the time? In what ways has their understanding grown over the years? Your teens will show a wide range of awareness about communion. What was the experience like for your students when *they* took communion for the first time?

DISCUSSION

1. Discuss student answers. Does the church eat together regularly? Can you describe those occasions? What foods are always present? Eating a regular meal (first daily in Acts 2:42, then weekly) was a regular practice of the early church.

2. Do your students have family conversation at meals, or are meals just for eating? Ask students if they have special meals for birthdays, Christmas, or Easter. What are they like? Do any of your students have special symbols or traditions at these meals? Are they connected to religious or ethnic traditions?

3. Let students share what they found. Jesus had evidently made some decisions and arranged for this special meal. The procedures for how to prepare the Passover were known by all, with specific timing for the sacrifice of the lamb. Jesus instructs Peter and John to prepare the meal, which involved obtaining the food and setting the room.

4. Each of the disciples, except Judas, calls Jesus "Lord," demonstrating their faith. Judas refers to Jesus as "Rabbi," a more formal name for a disciple to call his or her master. None of the disciples immediately assume it's Judas—this is clear because they ask if it's them. What did your students answer for the first question? If Jesus were to say to your group that one of them would be a betrayer, how would your students respond? How is disobedience similar to or different from betrayal?

5. Go over the questions and answers for this question. Read Paul's interpretation in 1 Corinthians 11:23-26. Ask students how Matthew 26:29 shows that Jesus is already looking into the future and past his coming death and resurrection? Read 1 Corinthians 15:20-25. What has Christ done that gives him power? Ask students to share what song or hymn they would've chosen to sing if they were leaving this last supper.

CLOSE

You, or a pastor, can conduct a short communion service at the end of your program if you have the time to do it well. If not, you can focus on the idea of remembrance. When your students want to remind themselves of God, who he is, and what he's done, what do they do? Do they have symbols or activities that are particularly helpful in remembering? Remind students that there's a danger when the symbol becomes more important that the One it's supposed to remind them of. Tell students you're going to do what the disciples did on that night—sing a hymn and then leave. Pick one of the songs mentioned by the students, one that most would know, and sing it together without music. Then dismiss your students quietly. Consider making this dismissal reflective and have the group either singing as they leave, reflecting on what Jesus has done for them—or leaving in near-silence as the 11 disciples might have done that evening after the Passover meal.

MORE

• **For more Scriptures about the Lord's Supper, see Paul's interpretation in 1 Corinthians 11:23-26. The bread usually symbolized God's blessing and provision (Matthew 14:9 and 15:36). How is Jesus' death and resurrection a blessing and provision for us? The cup was the third cup of the Passover, a cup of thanksgiving and blessing (1 Corinthians 10:16). What blessing should we be thankful for when we take communion? The phrase "blood of the new covenant" was prophesied in Jeremiah 31:31-34, the passage known as the "new covenant."**

• **The opening would be a great time to hand out copies of your church's understanding of communion, or information from churches that practice it.**

• **There are some resources online that explain what's involved with a Passover meal. Some of the symbolism of the Passover was used by Jesus with his disciples. Show parts of an online 40-minute video, "Christ in the Passover," found at video.google.com/videoplay?docid =5272606142394767394), or buy it at store.jewsforjesus.org/ppp/product.php?prodid=4.**

1. Get with two or three others around you. Which of the people in your group would make the best judge? Lawyer? Convict?

UNJUSTLY ACCUSED
The arrest and trial of Jesus
(Luke 22:47-23:5)

2. Still in your groups, complete the following: The events of Jesus' arrest and sentencing are listed in the probable order of how they happened. To the right of each item, put the letter of the passage that describes that event.

Jesus betrayed by Judas and arrested. _____

A. Matthew 27:27-31

Jesus tried by the Sanhedrin at night. _____

B. Mark 15:15

Jesus beaten by the religious guards. _____

C. John 18:1-8

Jesus before Pilate at daybreak. _____

D. John 19:4-16

Jesus before Herod. _____

E. Matthew 26:59-66

Jesus before Pilate again—and condemned. _____

F. Matthew 27:11-20

Jesus flogged. _____

G. Luke 22:63-65

Roman soldiers mock and beat Jesus. _____

H. Luke 23:8-12

3. Based on what Jesus says and how he acts during his trial, his endurance of physical abuse and mockery from his creation, how would you characterize his reactions? What's his message?

4. Read John 18:37-38. Imagine Pilate asks you the question, "What is truth?" What do you say truth is?

What is Pilate's verdict in verse 38?

Based on that verdict, what does Pilate do (19:15-16)?

5. Which of the following best describes your reactions when you think about Jesus' trial and death?

____ I get angry at the injustices that were done.

____ It makes me sad that he had to go through that.

____ I realize how serious sin is to God.

____ I'm reminded of how much God loves me and wants me to live for him.

____ I want to share the good news of what Jesus has done with others.

From *High School TalkSheets: 50 Ready-to-Use Discussions on the Life of Christ* by Terry Linhart. Permission to reproduce this page granted only for use in buyer's youth group. Copyright © 2009 by Youth Specialties. www.youthspecialties.com

THIS WEEK

This TalkSheet acquaints students with the events leading up to the crucifixion.

OPENER

Record an episode from one of the many TV programs featuring a judge, such as *Judge Judy*. Find an appropriate, entertaining, and funny section of two to three minutes to show. Find the cue and be able to quickly get to the judge's verdict. Tell students what the charges are against the plaintiff and then show your two- to three-minute section of the video to start the discussion. Ask your students if this is realistic and representative of a real courtroom. What do they think the verdict will be? Show the judge's verdict. Transition by asking students if this was a fair trial.

DISCUSSION

1. Who would make good judges from each of your groups? How about lawyers? Convicts? How did your groups determine who would be what? Ask those who were chosen as convicts by others in the group how they feel about that. Jesus was crucified among thieves and didn't receive a fair trial process. Jesus knew he would be betrayed, arrested, abused, and crucified. Ask your students to share what they think Jesus was thinking during those last hours. What does this say to us about God's view of sin?

2. Go through the answers to this so that everyone eventually gets them right. What did your students notice as they read these passages? How many trials did Jesus have? There's actually a sixth one with Annas (John 18:1-8) that isn't on this list. This process probably broke a number of Jewish laws (arrested at night, taken to the home of a religious leader, tried at night, and convicted on the same day). Why would the religious leaders break so many of their own laws? What does their willingness to break religious laws say about them?

3. What did your students conclude? Spend some time here and have people share what they wrote. Follow up with any comments needing clarification or possessing good insights. Remind students that it's difficult for us because we weren't there, and that words on a page can make it very sterile. If we were there and able to watch the proceedings, what would we see that isn't communicated through words? In what ways might our understanding of the crucifixion be affected?

4. What are your students' answers to the question "What is truth?" If 1 Peter 3:15 is our reminder, how prepared are we to give an answer to others about what truth is? About who Jesus is?

5. From the beginning (Genesis 3:15) and throughout the prophets of the Old Testament, this moment had been predicted—the moment when the Messiah would come and be the sacrifice for the sins of men and women. How *should* we respond to this message of what Christ has done? What do the words of Matthew 16:24-25 ("Whoever wants to be my disciple must deny themselves and take up their cross and follow me. For whoever wants to save their life will lose it, but whoever loses their life for me will find it.") challenge us to do?

CLOSE

Point out that it can be easy to overlook the great pain and humiliation Jesus endured before he was crucified. Remind your students that Jesus said the world would hate his followers (Matthew 10:22 and John 15:18-19). Ask students to react to that. Do they really think this is true? Jesus went one step further and said that we're to do good to those that hate us (Luke 6:22). Work with your students by discussing the idea that the world hates and persecutes Christians, but that we're still to be reflective of Christ's love to them.

MORE

• **For further Bible study, have students focus on the disciples in this story. What was their reaction (Mark 14:50)? Why did they disappear? What did Peter do in the garden (John 18:10)? Later, in the priest's courtyard (Luke 22:54-62; John 18:15-18, 25-27)? Was it dangerous for Peter to have followed Jesus so closely at this point? What do your students think Pilate thought about Jesus (Matthew 27:11-26; John 18:28-19:16)?**

• **A peripheral topic could be about the persecution Christians are currently enduring. You can get some resources at www.missionresources.com/persecuted. html and visit the Voice of the Martyrs' Web site at www. persecution.com.**

1. Write a definition for each of the following words:

     Redemption—

     Reconciliation—

THE ULTIMATE SACRIFICE
The death of Jesus on the cross
(Matthew 27:27-58)

2. Read Matthew 27:27-31. Jesus had just been severely whipped. What was the purpose of what the soldiers were doing?

In what ways do you see people mock Jesus today?

3. Look up Luke 23:40-43 and 47. What happened to each of these men?

Do you think the centurion was among those mocking Jesus? Why or why not?

4. Read Matthew 27:45-54. List the supernatural events that occurred at the time of Jesus' death.

5. Read 2 Corinthians 5:16-21 and, from those verses, complete the following statements about us.

     From now on, we regard…

     If anyone is in Christ…

     All of this is from God, who…

     God was reconciling the world…

     He has committed to us…

THIS WEEK

The central scene in the life of Christ was his death and resurrection. Despite the abundance of crosses on jewelry, the crucifixion isn't something most students talk about. This TalkSheet exposes students to the events of Jesus' death and reminds them of why Jesus died and what has been gained through his death and resurrection.

OPENER

Option A. If appropriate for your group, you can show the crucifixion scene from either *The Gospel of John* or *Jesus of Nazareth*. It's probably best to preview your chosen scenes first. Following the movie, lead a discussion by asking your students what they noticed in the movie. How realistic was it?

Option B. If you can't show the movie, ask students to remember a famous person who died suddenly. Have students share as many as they can remember. How did they react to the news? Ask students which of these people they'll remember the longest. Why? Read Matthew 27:27-55.

What were the reactions of the people: The crowd? The people raised from the dead? The Roman centurion? The woman watching from a distance? Where would your students have been on that day?

Have someone read 1 John 2:2. Tell students that Christ's death is called the atonement. Remind students that Jesus Christ was our substitute, offering himself as a sacrifice in our place so we could have forgiveness of sins and a right relationship with God.

DISCUSSION

1. Have students share their definitions for "redeem." Read Luke 4:16-19. What kind of redemption is God promising through Jesus? Have students share their definitions of reconciliation. Read 2 Corinthians 5:16-19. What are the effects of the reconciliation God gives to us? Who sinned and was wrong? Who initiated the reconciliation of the relationship?

2. The word used for the centurion means to "keep on glorifying." It's quite possible this wasn't a one-time thought about God, but a change in his faith. It's interesting that the first person to declare who Jesus was after his death was a Roman Gentile, a further indication that God's redemption and reconciliation was for the whole world through Jesus Christ.

3. The forgiveness of the thief on the cross and the confession of the Roman Centurion reveal Jesus' great love, compassion, and holiness. Even as he endured brutality, ridicule, and rejection, he forgave those who beat him, he loved the sinner and extended forgiveness, and he reacted to his executioners with love as Creator. What are the implications for us today? In what ways do we need to learn how to show God's grace and forgiveness?

4. Focus students' attention on the curtain tearing. Have someone look up and read Exodus 26:33. Have another look up and read Hebrews 9:2-3, 7. Ask students to share the purpose, symbolism, and rules of the curtain. The curtain reminded them of the holiness of God and their unrighteous nature. They would never be holy enough to be in God's presence, and even the high priest could only go in once a year. Ask students what it meant that the curtain tore when Jesus died. How could people have access to God's presence through Christ?

5. Go over these with your students, letting them share their answers. Ask students how God could accomplish all this (verse 21). What is it we're to do (verses 16 and 20)? What does it mean to regard people from a worldly point of view? What does it mean to be righteous? Is it difficult to think we can be declared righteous?

CLOSE

Have students look up Isaiah 53:7-9 and follow along with you as you read it aloud. Ask students to share how the various statements from these verses were true from what you discovered in this lesson. After a few minutes of discussion, have students close their eyes for a time of reflection. Remind them of God's immense love for his people and even though we were the ones who sinned against him, he sent his Son Jesus to stand in our place. That is really an incredible act that's very difficult for us to comprehend. Read Isaiah 53:7-9 again and then close in prayer.

MORE

• **Have students turn to Titus 3:4-7. Why did God choose to save us? According to this passage, how does God save us? Luke 23:39-43 is the story of the two thieves crucified on either side of Christ. In John 10:17-18, Jesus said that no one could take his life from him, but that he would lay it down willingly—and John 19:31-33 confirmed that.**

• **Write John 15:12-13 on the board: "My command is this: Love each other as I have loved you. Greater love has no one than this: to lay down one's life for one's friends." Christ modeled a principle of what it means to be Christian—that we love others by laying down our lives. When is that the easiest to do? The most difficult? Is it hard to lay down your life at home for your siblings? If we went to your friends and asked how well you do at this, what might they say? Help your students develop some steps they can put in place for the next week to help them grow in their Christlikeness.**

1. Do you think UFOs exist? Why or why not?

What would it take for you to believe that UFOs exist? Rank the following forms of proof from least convincing (1) to most convincing (6).

___ More than three people saw it at different times.
___ Reading about it in the newspaper.
___ Seeing video of it on the Internet or TV.
___ Seeing one yourself.
___ A teacher at school says they could exist based on mathematical probabilities in the universe.
___ Getting on board a UFO and flying around the world.

HE'S ALIVE!
The resurrection of Jesus
(Matthew 28:1-4; Luke 24:1-35; John 20:10-29; 1 Corinthians 15:3-8)

2. Read Matthew 28:1-4 and Luke 24:1-12. List two or three reasons the angels said what they said to the women.

What was the disciples' reaction to the women's story?

3. Pick one of the following stories to read: (1) Luke 24:13-24 and 28-35; (2) John 20:10-18; or (3) John 10:24-31. Imagine you're a reporter for the local Jerusalem newspaper and you've interviewed the people in the story. Describe the following;

Whom did Jesus appear to?

What were their feelings before they encountered Jesus?

How did they know it was Jesus?

What do they believe now about Jesus?

4. Read 1 Corinthians 15:3-7. List the people Paul says Jesus appeared to after his resurrection.

5. When you think of what it means to be a Christian, which of the following biblical images are the most meaningful to you? Circle the top two.

Baptism	Lord's Supper/Eucharist	Washing feet	Jesus' healing
The cross	The empty tomb	Pentecost	The Good Shepherd

THIS WEEK

The resurrection of Jesus Christ was the ultimate demonstration of God's power over sin and death. Jesus showed that he was not only a great teacher and healer, but also the Son of God, alive today. The accounts of those who first saw Jesus after his resurrection give us glimpses of how grief was turned into joy as the reality of this truth set in. The resurrection is not only a great story, but a present reality for us today. Christ appeared to many people after his resurrection and these appearances connect to students' lives as they consider the role of the risen Christ in their life today.

OPENER

Have students share what Easter traditions they remember from their childhood. Try to get a full range of answers—did they go to an early church service? Eat certain food? Go on egg hunts? Give gifts? Dress up? Ask what "stories" these events tell. The early disciples told a story of Jesus' resurrection. Have three different students read Acts 2:1-12; 6:8-15; and 7:51-60. What are the main themes of these stories? What are the main points they want to make about Jesus' resurrection?

DISCUSSION

1. This question gets students to think about what it must've been like for those who saw the resurrected Jesus and then reported it to others. Have students imagine that they were a skeptical person who didn't believe Jesus had risen from the dead and then met him face to face. How would that affect how you told others about Jesus in the future? What's the difference between someone claiming to see a UFO and those who encountered the risen Son of God?

2. Why is it significant that Jesus is no longer dead? What did it mean for the women and the 12 disciples that Jesus was alive? Does it mean the same for us today, or is it different? Why?

3. This question will take students some time to finish, so make sure to give them time to share what they wrote. What feelings are present in the story? How were their lives changed because of this encounter?

4. Why was it important for Paul to list these various encounters? Read 1 Corinthians 15:14: "And if Christ has not been raised, our preaching is useless and so is your faith." What's Paul saying here about the resurrection?

5. Have students share the ones that mean the most to them. All of them are important, so don't let them be ranked in importance. Most Christians in America think of the cross as the important symbol in this list. How might the empty tomb be an equally powerful symbol? How does the empty tomb give more power to what Christ did on the cross?

CLOSE

Have students close their eyes and imagine they were alive at the time of Christ. It has been many days after Jesus' death and they're walking through Jerusalem where Simon Peter, one of Jesus' followers, is preaching. There's excitement in the crowd gathered here in the town. Read Acts 2:22-41 as if Peter is addressing your students. Ask them whether they think this message is still as urgent today or not. What does Peter say is to be our response?

MORE

• There are many great resources online regarding the resurrection. Josh McDowell has done an extensive amount of work to equip youth workers and students with resources. He has a Web page on the resurrection at www.leaderu.com/everystudent/easter/articles/josh2.html. You can also check more resources on his Web site at www.beyondbelief.com/r_apologetics.spl. If you want to use some of the apologetics materials, they would fit well as you discuss question #4.

• If you want to focus students more on what it must have been like for the early Christians, you can draw some parallels to UFO sightings. There are some great UFO sighting stories online—one at Chicago O'Hare airport in 2006 and another in Stephensville, Texas, in 2008—and you can show them to students to see how they react.

1. In your opinion, why did Peter deny he knew Jesus?

2. Have you ever been in a situation where you denied knowing someone? How did that make you feel afterward?

3. In pairs, read John 21:15-19. What does Jesus challenge Peter to do?

How does the number of times Jesus challenges Peter correspond with Peter's denials?

4. Read Luke 24:34 and 1 Corinthians 15:5. Jesus probably forgave Peter privately, so why did Jesus challenge him publicly?

5. Read the following verses. What role did Peter end up having in the early church? How does that encourage you?

Matthew 16:13-20   Acts 2:37-42   Acts 4:8-15

THIS WEEK

Peter, the one God would build his church on, actually denied Jesus during his greatest need. But Peter found forgiveness and was still used in mighty ways to lead the early church. This TalkSheet gives students the opportunity to understand that they too can be forgiven and used by God in mighty ways.

OPENER

Take three students aside and give them each a playing card. Make sure one of the three cards is the ace of hearts. Have the students memorize their card, then put it in their pocket. Instruct the three students to stand in front of the rest of the students and take turns denying they have the ace of hearts. Ask the group of students which person they believe actually has the ace of hearts. If they're correct, have that student show the card. If not, have the student who really had the ace of hearts show the card.

Inform the students that this week they'll be learning about how the apostle Peter denied having known and been with Jesus, but also how Jesus restored him later. Have one student with a good voice read Matthew 26:31-35 and another student read Matthew 26:69-74.

DISCUSSION

1. This is a fairly straightforward question, though you might be surprised at some of the answers your students will give. Give students time to answer in front of the group, and feel free to follow up their answers with more questions about why they said what they did.

2. Almost everyone has denied knowing someone else at some point. This could be an embarrassing or hurtful memory in students' lives. Tell students that denying people is unfortunately a common event in most people's lives, and they shouldn't feel like they're the only ones who have done it. Encourage them to remember how it felt to deny someone else to help them see why they don't want to do it again. Usually guilt is the most common emotion experienced.

3. Break students into pairs. Jesus questioned Peter three times, asking Peter if he loves him. Each time Jesus followed up the question by challenging him to "feed my lambs" and "take care of my sheep." What do these challenges mean to the students? The second question deals with Peter's public restoration.

Since Peter denied Jesus three times, Jesus had Peter confess his love for Jesus publicly three times. After this, no one questioned Peter's authority or commitment to Jesus.

4. It's believed that since Jesus had met with Peter before the time Peter was challenged publicly, forgiveness and restoration had already taken place between the two. It's important to remember that sins against one person should be dealt with between those two people, not out in public for everyone to see. Perhaps the reason Jesus did both in the case of Peter was not only to restore Peter publicly, but also to show that no matter what a person does, he or she can still be forgiven. This can be a huge encouragement to students.

5. Peter was the Rock, the foundation of the church. Jesus was planning this even though he knew Peter would deny him. In Acts there are countless examples of Peter's proclaiming the gospel of Jesus Christ. We see that Peter could be used in mighty ways for Christ. It's encouraging to know that no matter what we do, we can be forgiven and even be used by God in mighty ways.

CLOSE

This story is not as much about Peter's denial as it is about his restoration. Jesus died on the cross for all our sins, and when we find forgiveness through him, we can be sure we've been restored. Post the following verses up front: 1 John 1:9; 2 Corinthians 5:17; and Galatians 2:20. Have three students with good voices stand up and read the verses. Then give each student an index card and pen and tell them to copy the verse that means the most to them now. Challenge them to memorize that verse over the next week.

MORE

This is a great time to have students not only think through past times when they denied someone, but also consider approaching them to ask for forgiveness for it. Give students a few minutes to pray about who they might need to ask forgiveness from, and then challenge them to do it after the program is over. Another possibility to bring up is the student who needs to forgive another person for denying them, even if the other person hasn't asked for forgiveness. A lot of personal healing could come through this time.

(Thanks to Tom Carpenter for the TalkSheet idea)

1. If I were asked to read something I enjoyed, I'd choose (circle one letter):

a. A story that's an allegory of some larger truth.
b. A favorite poem I hadn't read yet.
c. A science-fiction book.
d. A fictional story set in today's society.
e. A nonfiction work about a historical theme.
f. A magazine.
g. Instructions for something I recently purchased.

2. There is an area of study called eschatology, which means "the study of last things." Answer the following questions:

What is your belief about the world's future?

Will it end?

If so, what are the last things you think will happen?

How far into the future do you think it will end?

3. Look up any two of the following passages and read them. Write down what they say will happen in the future.

> Matthew 24:29-30—
> John 14:3—
> Acts 1:10-11—
> 1 Thessalonians 2:19—

4. Jesus said in Matthew 24:36 - 25:13 that he could come back at any hour. Quickly read those verses and write down the reactions he says people will have.

5. Which of the following best characterizes what you've learned about the end times (pick one)? How far into the future?

❑ **There will be a rapture, then seven years of tribulation.**
❑ **Christ will come back after a time of tribulation and reign on earth for a millennium.**
❑ **Daniel and Revelation are allegorical and talk about the church age of Pentecost.**
❑ **The events of Revelation have happened in history and are happening now.**
❑ **All the signs of the end times have been fulfilled and we're now waiting for Christ's return.**

THIS WEEK

End times is a topic students often like to study—it's mysterious, exciting, and yet an area of fear as well. It's also a topic that, depending on the denomination, has a wide range of views. All throughout history, Christians looked at current events and were convinced they were living in the end times. This lesson focuses on the foundational biblical themes regarding end times. You may need to do a little background study on end times, as this topic generally brings out the questions!

OPENER

Tell students that the end times is an area of the Bible in which people have a wide range of views, and each person usually thinks they have interpreted it correctly. This TalkSheet focuses on the foundational biblical themes regarding the end times. Ask students who are indifferent about end-time topics to raise their hands. Then, have students who would say they're concerned about end-time topics to raise their hands. Then, ask those who are somewhere in the middle to raise their hands. Should people care to know about these topics? Tell students you're going to be talking about end times. Ask students to shout out questions they may have about the end times and write those on the board. You may want to deal with those as you go through this lesson or come back to them next week and provide answers then.

DISCUSSION

1. Have the students divide into seven groups based on what they picked. Have them line up in order so that your A group is on one end and the G group on the other. You will have some groups without members and that's fine. Have students share why they like the type of reading they picked, making sure to get as many students to share as possible. Ask, "Is there a range in place here from one end to the other?" Allow students to interact with each other about this. Tell students the A group is fond of allegory, the B group poetry, while the G group likes to read technical writing (instructions). If we prefer different kinds of readings, do people then read the Bible differently? How are we to read a book like Revelation? Daniel? Some read it more literally than others and this leads to the various perspectives about a key, difficult part of Christian theology.

2. Encourage students to share their answers about end times. Follow up by asking whether thinking about end times makes them fearful or hopeful.

3. All four of these passages declare that Jesus is coming again, an event described as universal. What does *universal* mean? Do your students think people are aware of the biblical prophecy that Jesus is coming back?

4. Ask students to share what they wrote. A subtle part of these stories is that when Jesus comes back, it'll be too late to respond to God's love and gospel. When your students think about Jesus coming back, are they hopeful or fearful? Ask students, "When does eternal life begin for a Christian?" Does it begin at salvation, or at the end of this life? If it's the latter, the danger is that we spend our days merely watching and waiting. If eternal life begins when we put our faith in Christ, then it starts now, and we can live in the kingdom of God now and make a difference now.

5. Each of these views represents different ways that Christians who read through the same Bible think about the end times. Which of these seems the strangest to you? Which one did most of your students select? Ask your students how they learned about their particular view of the end times.

CLOSE

The most-repeated truths about end times is that (a) Jesus is coming back, (b) he could do so at any hour, and (c) it will be a universal and final event. Remind your students that all throughout history, Christians have looked at events of their day and thought they were in the end times. Is it easy to get too content and not live our lives as though Jesus could come back at any hour? Ask students to summarize what you talked about during this TalkSheet regarding the end times. Ask students to imagine—not answering out loud—that tonight will be the evening when Jesus comes back. What would their response be? What does that response indicate? Close with prayer that your students will live their lives as if Jesus is coming back any day.

MORE

• **You may want to teach your students some of the major terms associated with end times. You can find a "Jeopardy PowerPoint" online (Google it!). Then Google "eschatology glossary" for Web sites that'll give you the various terms associated with end-time theology. Divide your group into three teams and play the game with them, a helpful and fun way to have students interact with the major terms.**

• **For more passages on the end times, you can have students study Daniel 9:20-27; 12:1-4; Zechariah 14:1-5; Matthew 24:1-28; 2 Thessalonians 2:1-12; 1 John 2:18-19; and Revelation 20:1-10. If you're leading a church group, you'll need to get a copy of your church's doctrine of end times that will help them see how these passages and others apply.**